Young in the Twenties

BY THE SAME AUTHOR

The author, so young in the Twenties . . .   *(E. O. Hoppé)*

ETHEL MANNIN

Young in the Twenties

A CHAPTER OF AUTOBIOGRAPHY

HUTCHINSON OF LONDON

HUTCHINSON & CO (*Publishers*) LTD
178–202 Great Portland Street, London W1

London Melbourne Sydney
Auckland Johannesburg Cape Town
and agencies throughout the world

First published 1971

© Ethel Mannin 1971

*This book has been set in Baskerville type, printed in Great Britain
on antique wove paper by Anchor Press, and
bound by Wm. Brendon, both of Tiptree, Essex*

ISBN 0 09 107100 3

To my old friend
PAUL TANQUERAY
who was young with me
in the Twenties

Acknowledgments

Many people have helped me with this book, one way and another—with suggestions, reminders, the loan of books, odd bits of research—and I am very grateful to them all, but outstandingly to my old friend, Paul Tanqueray, without whose patient and devoted assistance the book could hardly have been written. I owe a great debt of gratitude, also, to John Walters, who spent a day in Fleet Street going through newspaper files on my behalf; to my Borough Librarian friend, Gilbert Turner, who, as always, supplied books and patiently dealt with endless queries; to 'Tim' Ziemsen and John Foster White for assistance with proofs; to Vincent Sheehan for permission to quote from his book, *In Search of History*; to Godfrey Winn for the use of his photograph of some of us at one of his parties in the early Thirties; and to Dr. W. Lindesay Neustatter for the photograph of his mother, 'Mrs. Lins'.

E.M.

Contents

Illustrations

PART I

The 'Scene'

I

Young and uppity

On January 1, 1920, I was just over nineteen years old, newly married, pregnant, working in the London advertising agency to which I had gone in the summer of 1916, at the age of fifteen, and living in furnished rooms in Strawberry Hill, Middlesex, with my husband, who was a copy-writer in the same agency, to which he had returned after having been 'demobbed'. Whatever was happening in that brand-new decade I was not much interested in it, being too busy Living My Life. More important than the events in India and Ireland at that time was the fact that I was married, 'expecting', and beginning to establish myself as a free-lance journalist. Of all this I wrote in my youthful *Confessions and Impressions*, written in 1929 and published in 1930, and there is no point in repeating it here; what I am concerned with here is filling in the lacunae in that rash and brash account—the blanks which when filled in present something of the 'scene' of that extraordinary decade of the Twenties and what it meant to be young and at large in it.

That the *Confessions*, so daringly outspoken at the time, and a *succès de scandale*, takes no account of the scene is not surprising; the scene is unremarkable when you are yourself part of it; it is simply the way things are. We who were young in the Twenties are intensely aware of the Seventies' scene because we have no part in it—nor want any; it is not our world;

our world folded up at the end of the Thirties; the Twenties, with their surface gaiety, their self-conscious—and conscientious—audacity, and their genuine enthusiasms and excitements—a great deal really was 'mah'vlous' then—were our final fling.

We didn't know it, of course. We only knew that the war-to-end-wars was fought and won; that is to say we believed that it was, just as we believed that the world had been 'made safe for democracy'. The very young among us, such as I was, didn't think much about it. The war, during which we had grown up, was over. There had been the Armistice 'high jinks' —it was an expression we used—and for the serious-minded there was the problem of something called 'Reconstruction', and for the young and light-minded there was 'fun'. *'Ain't we got fun?'* was a line in a popular song. It was a sardonic song, to be sure, but still we liked it, we sang it, we danced to it, kicking up our heels. We were *gay*; not a doubt of it. We laughed a lot, we danced a lot, we told each other *risqué* stories—there are no such stories nowadays, for when all is permitted how be *risqué*? The word itself is as dated as 'saucy', which preceded it. We used to ask each other, at parties, and places where they meet, 'Heard any good stories lately?' Mostly they were fairly funny; sometimes they were crude; but we liked them, and wondered who invented them, and they kept a party going. We hooted with laughter; we were easily amused, and, with all the sophistication and promiscuity, sentimental.

We loved Delysia, all diamanté and ostrich feathers singing, sweetly :

> *'If you could care for me*
> *As I could care for you-oo.'*

It was as simple as that. We were a very believing generation. Unashamedly we could declare of love at first sight, in the words of another popular song :

'I took one look at you,
That's all I meant to do;
And then my heart stood still.'

Piquant little Jessie Matthews sang it in a Cochran revue
in 1927; it was charming, tender, haunting; she sang it very
sweetly, with Richard Dolman.

I celebrated my twenty-first birthday, in October, 1921,
with a small dinner party at the Holborn Restaurant—of
course a dinner-dance, for we reckoned to dance between
courses. My husband and I had a little more elbow room,
financially, by that time; he had 'got on' in the advertising
agency, and I was making about twenty pounds a month with
women's page articles in the London and provincial press, and
the odd half-guinea here and there for sentimental-romantic
verses in magazines—one was called the *Blue Magazine*, and
all its stories were of romantic love; I was also writing thirty-
thousand-word novelettes at a guinea a thousand, with such
sultry titles as *Bruised Wings*, and *The Tinsel Eden*, and though
I aspired to be an authoress, as it was then called, not just a
journalist, this had not yet happened. Meanwhile the money
I earned by this journalism enabled me to put down money
to furnish the semi-detached house for which my husband had
been able to put down the deposit for the mortgage. It also
enabled us to have a Saturday night fling in a restaurant with
dancing—at old Romano's in the Strand, or Prince's in
Piccadilly. And a resident maid, a 'cook general', who considered herself well paid with thirty shillings a week and 'all
found'—many people only paid twenty-five. Cap and apron,
of course; blue cotton dress in the mornings, black cloth in the
afternoons—and coffee-coloured caps and aprons were just
that much smarter than plain white ones. This resident maid,
who was always very young, did all the housework, the cook-
ing, a certain amount of washing and ironing, and took the
baby out in the afternoons. She had an afternoon and evening
off once a week, and every other Sunday after lunch. The man
of the house was always referred to as the Master, and the
mistress addressed as Madam. It was snobbish; it was class

B

distinction; it was exploitation; but it worked. That is to say there was never any shortage of such labour, and any maid not happy in her employment could leave in the full confidence of getting another job easily enough. In the late Thirties I met behind the counter in a local shop a woman who had been one of my maids in the Twenties; we chatted and talked about the 'old days', and I told her I considered I had been a shocking young snob in those days, giving myself absurd airs which it embarrassed me now to remember. She replied, warmly, 'Oh, no, Madam! You were sweet!'

I am quite sure that I wasn't, but young and uppity; all the same I am glad she remembered me like that. I probably gave her ten bob at Christmas, and the occasional dress I was tired of. Quite intensely I dislike the memory of myself when young; but it's the way I was. I was of my times; quintessentially.

I achieved my ambition of becoming an 'authoress' when I was twenty-two. I wrote an earnest novel which I called *Martha*, about a girl who 'loved not wisely but too well', as it was delicately put at that time, and who had the misfortune to have an illegitimate child. I entered it for a first-novel competition, and it came in second and was duly published by Leonard Parsons in 1923, with an attractive jacket depicting Leicester Square with the old Alhambra music-hall. The artist was John Armstrong. I was then Ethel E. Mannin. There was, after all, a very famous woman novelist called Ethel M. Dell, so why not Ethel E. Mannin? I was no less entitled to the use of my second baptismal name.

In his book *The Nineteen Twenties*, published in 1945, the late Douglas Goldring describes how for four pounds a week he was engaged by the literary agents, J. B. Pinker, 'to weed out the MSS sent in for this competition', and how he 'spotted Ethel Mannin's first novel as a potential winner . . . and she became in consequence one of his most valued authors'. That I met Douglas Goldring as a result of his reading the typescripts of the first novels entered for this competition I have myself recorded in *Confessions*, but this first novel and all my early work was handled not by Pinker but by the equally distinguished literary agents, Curtis Brown. Pinker was never more than a name to me, and with Curtis Brown, who numbered many famous authors among their clients, I was not more—or less—'cherished' than any other promising young writer for whom they acted. It must have been Curtis Brown who organised the competition, or how would I have come to be one of their authors? It is evident that writing after more than twenty years Goldring's memory misgave him. I am only sorry that in *The Nineteen Twenties* he makes no reference to the warm friendship which developed, though by the time he wrote it had lapsed and I did not know of the publication of the book. Why it lapsed I have long forgotten, and when, but we were still friends when I wrote my second volume of autobiography, *Privileged Spectator*, in 1938, in which I wrote of him as one of my oldest friends; so perhaps it was the War, which cut across so many friendships, which came between us. He does mention, however, that I was one of the people who visited him and his second wife during the two years they were living in the South of France, at Juan-les-Pins—I, in fact, stayed with them in their apartment, in August, 1928, when he gave me an affectionately inscribed copy of his poems, *Streets*, published in 1920.

I admired Douglas Goldring very much as a critic, and as a writer of ideas and integrity, but I am quite sure he was a very poor poet; some of the verses in *Streets*, however, do convey the contemporary scene:

> '*In friendly restaurant or grill*
> *You drink your bottle, eat your fill,*
> *Digest, while watching Russian dancers,*
> *Drive next to supper at some pub,*
> *Then mingle with the rag-time prancers,*
> *In a night café—called a club.*'

Goldring himself was very much of the period, and enjoyed the first half of the decade enormously, as he tells us in his book. He was about ten years my senior, and in those days young writers looked up to the older ones. He was important to me as the first fellow-author I ever met. I had already met

Gilbert Frankau, at the country house of Charles Higham, the
famous advertising agent for whom I had worked for nearly
five years, and for whom my husband still worked, but as the
best-selling author of the novel, *Peter Jackson, Cigar Merchant,*
he was so far beyond the young free-lance journalist I was
then that it would have been presumptuous to have thought
of him as a fellow-author.

With the publication of *Martha* I was interviewed by the
Daily Sketch, which seemed to me then the height of celebrity.
I was taken up on to the roof of the *Sketch* building and photographed. The interviewer was good enough to say that the
novel was a 'remarkable achievement for a girl of twenty-
two'. It wasn't, of course; it was merely a good try, and the
sixth-form mistress of the elementary school at which I finished
my formal education at the age of fourteen, and who had
taken an interest in me because I was so good at 'composition',
told me some years later how bitterly disappointed she had
been in that first novel; it had seemed to her so very 'ordinary'
—which it was. But in 1929 Jarrolds, who had by then published five novels from me, reprinted it in a 'new and revised
edition'. I can't think why, or of what the revisions consisted.

My second novel, *Hunger of the Sea,* was published by
Jarrolds in their Jay Library at the end of 1924, with a jacket
designed by Laura Knight, a strong charcoal drawing of fisher-
men. The setting of the novel was the fishing quarter of old
Hastings—which I still love—and the influence behind its
reaction was the earth-earthy novels of Knut Hamsun, who
was having a vogue here at that time. It was a distinct improvement on *Martha*, and it was flattering to be in the Jay Library,
edited by Benn Levy, as the literary standard was high and
the list included André Gide. The novel was published at the
then standard price of seven-and-six, and there was a limited
and numbered edition on handmade paper at thirty shillings
—a distinction in which at the time I was singularly little interested, which I now find astonishing. With this novel I
dropped the middle initial from my name and became plain
Ethel Mannin, it having been pointed out to me that though
it was Ethel M. Dell it was plain Bill Shakespeare.

2

A view from the stalls

But the publication of those two novels was not the sole excitement of those first years of the Twenties, for in 1922 there was Barry Jackson's production of Rutland Boughton's opera, *The Immortal Hour*, which meant so fantastically much to my generation. With the evocation of the memory the words by Fiona Macleod (William Sharp), set to the haunting music of Rutland Boughton, run through my head, though it is forty-five years ago since those magic nights at the theatre—and there was magic then—when Gwen Ffrangcon-Davies as Etain, the lost princess of this Celtic legend, trailed on to the stage in her long dress, with her streaming hair entwined with mistletoe, singing to a slow monotonous air :

> '*I will go back*
> *To the Country of the Young,*
> *And see again*
> *The lances of the Shee . . .'*

Enter, then, through the dim wood, the dark figure of Dalua, Son of Shadow, brother of the immortal gods, led there by dreams and visions, hearing the footfall of predestined things. Etain becomes the wife of Eochaidh, High King of Ireland, but Midir, the shining one, a prince of the Hidden People, lures her away. It is he who sings the Fairy Song we all knew by heart, and bought records of for our hand-wound gramophones, and which now, more than half a lifetime later, runs through my head, unfalteringly, both words and music:

> '*How beautiful they are,*
> *The lordly ones*
> *Who dwell in the hills,*
> *In the hollow hills.*'

And the stirring last verse:

> '*They laugh and are glad*
> *And are terrible:*
> *When their lances shake*
> *Every green reed quivers.*
>
> *How beautiful they are,*
> *How beautiful,*
> *The lordly ones*
> *In the hollow hills.*'

But memory plays one tricks; I had remembered Midir standing there sheathed in shining gold, but getting out the volume of the poems and dramas of Fiona Macleod I see that he is described as 'clad all in green, with a gold belt, a gold torque round his neck, gold armlets on his bare arms, and two gold torques round his bare ankles. On his long curling dark hair, falling over his shoulder, is a small green cap from which trails a peacock feather.' But perhaps on the stage he was all gold; certainly he was the shining one, troubling the heart of Etain. He plays chess with the king and wins, and the agreed reward being his heart's desire he asks the king that he might touch with his lips 'the white hand of the queen'. It is when he has kissed her hand that he sings of the Lordly Ones, and then, in a Tristan and Isolde crescendo of passion, of love:

> '*I am a song*
> *In the land of the Young,*
> *A sweet song;*
> *I am Love.*

> *I am a bird*
> *With white wings*
> *And a breast of flame*
> *Singing, singing:'*

Then at the peak of ecstasy :

> '*Etain, Etain,*
> *My Heart's Desire;*
> *Love, love, love,*
> *Sorrow, Sorrow!'*

He offers her life and love, and spellbound she follows him, hearing only his luring song, going from dark to light, the anguished plea of Eochaidh not to leave him falling on her ears as 'strange forgotten words, already dumb'. When she and Midir have disappeared from sight, out of the shadows steps Dalua, and the king cries to him, 'My dreams! My dreams! Give me my dream!' Dalua replies, touching him, 'There is none left but this—the dream of Death.'

We came out of the theatre with our eyes unashamedly wet. We were not all gin-and-sin; we were romantic, too, our sophistication only skin-deep. We held hands at *The Immortal Hour* and identified ourselves with the rôles : we suffered. When it was revived in 1924 we saw it all over again, recapturing the enchantment.

But before that revival we had had another theatrical excitement—the spectacular production at His Majesty's Theatre of James Elroy Flecker's *Hassan*, with its tragic Oriental drama and its splendid erotic poetry :

> '*And some to Mecca turn to pray, and I toward thy bed,*
> *Yasmin.*'

That was daring stuff in those pre-Chatterley days, and powerfully dramatic in its rising passion, with the intimations of death :

> '*Shower down thy love, O burning bright! for one night*
> *or the other night*

*Will come the Gardener in white, and gathered flowers
are dead, Yasmin!'*

There was the unashamed romanticism, too, so that we
were not embarrassed but, on the contrary, moved, when
Hassan declared to Yasmin—a slut, if ever there was one—'I
am nothing and you are the Queen of the Stars of the Night.
But the thought of you is twisted in the strings of my heart; I
burn with love of you, Yasmin.'

The Procession of Protracted Death, and the young lovers
broken on the wheel, choosing death by torture rather than
separation, was most terrible to us, not conditioned, as nowadays, to violence of this order on the stage, and pure of television, and though we steeled ourselves to watch it, in the
name of poetry and dramatic art, we suffered—exquisitely.
Henry Ainley, a most handsome man, richly endowed with
what today is called charisma, and a fine dramatic actor, mag-
nificently portrayed Hassan, and the lovers were most beauti-
fully played by Laura Cowie and Basil Gill.

The Golden Road to Samarkand poem in *Hassan* made a
powerful impression on my young mind, though it was ten
years before I took that then forbidden road, travelling illegally to Turkestan, and subsequently writing the book which
made me henceforth *persona non grata* in the U.S.S.R., *South
to Samarkand*, published in 1936; though before then I had
published two novels with titles from that poem, *Men are
Unwise,* and *Women Also Dream* :

*'What would ye, ladies? It was ever thus.
Men are unwise and curiously planned.'*

A woman replies :

'They have their dreams, and do not think of us.'

And the voices of the caravan sing, retreating into the distance :

'We take the Golden Road to Samarkand.'

There was all that of romantic poetry, but there was also something which was exciting in its newness, Sutton Vane's play, *Outward Bound*, produced in 1923. The action took place aboard a liner, journeying through eternity, all of whose passengers are dead, though only one of them knows it. This was something quite sensational in its originality.

R. C. Sherriff's war play, *Journey's End*, with its all-male cast, first produced in London by the Stage Society, at the Apollo Theatre, on a Sunday night in December, 1928, was something we all went to see and enthused about, but I don't think it made the impact of *Outward Bound*. A young actor called Laurence Olivier played in it on the Sunday night and the following Monday matinée, and on the strength of these performances was engaged to play a leading part in *Beau Geste*, which was to go on at His Majesty's Theatre in a few weeks' time. In his autobiography, *No Leading Lady*, Sherriff wrote that Olivier had been magnificent in *Journey's End*, as Captain Stanhope, and that he couldn't imagine a production of the play without him. The following January Maurice Browne produced the play at the Savoy Theatre, with the same cast, except that Stanhope was now played by another un-known young actor, Colin Clive, who had recently had a small part in *Show Boat*, which Sherriff wrote, 'didn't sound very promising', but the moment he saw him, he added, 'I knew he was our man. His performance proved to be magnificent; more rugged and restrained than Olivier's, but deeply moving.'

Clive played Stanhope throughout the tremendously success-ful London run and made his name in it, and though he was not in the cast in America went to Hollywood later to play in the film, and became a star. The play had on Broadway the same sort of success it had had in London, with rave notices and full houses, and, Sherriff tells us, after such a 'smash hit' the film companies 'were on to the play like bees round a honey-pot'.

In London, after the Stage Society production, Hannen Swaffer—to Sherriff's great surprise—wrote in the *Daily Express* that *Journey's End* was perhaps the greatest of all war plays, and that it carried a lesson, and 'one that is nobly told.'

There were, of course, other interesting theatrical events; there was the great musical, *Rose Marie*, which seemed to go on forever, and there were the plays of Mr. Noël Coward; but I am concerned here only with what made an impact on the young person that was myself and what moved and stirred my own particular circle. Mr. Coward's cynical witticisms—as they then seemed—were no more for me than the lush romanticism of *Rose Marie*. I was probably wrong on both counts— but it's the way I was.

Rose Marie, with Derek Oldham as the handsome hero and lovely Edith Day as the heroine, ran for 851 performances, and the King, George V, went to see it four times. Leslie Baily has an interesting note on this,* for he records that Edith Day could not be presented to His Majesty 'because her marriage had been dissolved', and in the Twenties divorced people, even if they were 'the innocent party', did not meet royalty and were debarred from the royal enclosure at Ascot and from royal garden parties. Which is all very interesting in the light of what was to happen with the King himself, Edward VIII, in 1938.

A rising young writer called J. B. Priestley had given us his novel, *The Good Companions,* by 1929, but not his plays of a new dimension in time.

I never saw Nigel Playfair's revival of *The Beggar's Opera*, which ran at the Lyric Theatre, Hammersmith, from 1920 to 1923, perhaps because of my innate aversion to opera— though under the influence of a Wagnerite friend I surrendered, totally, to the power and the glory of the *Ring* cycle at Covent Garden in the summer of 1929.

A play I did see in 1923, however, and with considerable excitement, was Karel Capek's *R.U.R.*, the play which added the word 'robot' to the language. The initials which form the title for the play stand for Rossum's Universal Robots. Robots were factory-produced beings, highly intelligent but without emotions, designed for work. They develop an emotion eventually, hate, and turn against humans and set out to destroy

* In his *Scrapbook for the Twenties,* 1959

mankind. The play was written in 1921 and translated into English by Paul Selver in 1923. It was adapted for the English stage by Nigel Playfair and produced by Basil Dean at the St. Martin's Theatre, London, in April, 1923. It had a wonderful cast, with Leslie Banks as Radius, the chief male robot, Ian Hunter as Primus, a more 'human' robot, who, instead of learning to hate like Radius, learns to love, and falls in love with Helena, a beautiful female robot, designed to look as much as possible like Helena Glory, the daughter of Professor Glory of Oxbridge University. Helena Glory was played by Frances Carson, and the robot Helena by Olga Lindo. That gentlest and most charming of actors, C. V. France, played Dr. Gall, the Head of the Physiological and Experimental Department of R.U.R. The scene of the play is set 'on a remote island, 1950–60'. Re-reading the play now, in the computer age, it seems less sensational; in 1923 it was described in the theatre programme as 'A Fantastic Melodrama'; fantasy it was, but also, in a sense, prophecy. A German film, *Metropolis*, carried a similar message—the potentially destructive power of the machine, overwhelming Man, its creator. 'Metropolis' was the dehumanised, concrete jungle, skyscraper city of the future. Later, in the Thirties, we were to have Aldous Huxley's satirical novel, *Brave New World*, and H. G. Wells' gloomy *The Shape of Things to Come*, but in essence the Czech dramatist Karel Capek said it first in his play *R.U.R.*, in the early Twenties. His *Letters from England* were translated into English and published here in 1925.

It should perhaps be said here that *Metropolis* was not the first great German film of the Twenties, for in 1920 we experienced the excitement of the German impressionist film *The Cabinet of Dr. Caligari*, which was something really new in films, and as such a tremendous aesthetic and intellectual experience for us, enabling us to take the film seriously as *Art*—to which we always gave a capital A. We were fascinated by the long, dream-like perspectives, the sleep-walking sequence, by a sense of unreality that was nevertheless intensely real, with the reality of nightmare.

The theatre was an *occasion* in the Twenties; you 'dressed' for it, and your male escort wore at least a black tie and dinner-jacket; for a first night he probably wore white tie and tails. It was a lot of nonsense, but also it added to the gaiety. I was a considerable first-nighter. I expected to be recognised, and was. There was a woman journalist for one of the glossies who always looked out for me and wrote luscious gossipy para-graphs—'lovely Ethel Mannin, striking in black, with a huge pink ostrich feather fan'. Pink ostrich feathers! I can only repeat helplessly that it's the way I was. I must say, in passing, however, that it was a lovely dress for which the pink ostrich feather fan was an accessory—black chiffon over pink silk, with tiny pink silk rosebuds stitched to tiers of flounces. I saw it advertised in a theatre programme and went next day to buy it. Not all the Twenties fashions were ugly and silly, by any means; towards the end of the decade, when femininity be-came fashionable again, many of the evening dresses were graceful and charming. 'Gracious living' is a contemporary phrase, associated with central heating and double-glazed windows, but I think we knew more about it in the Twenties, when we had a sense of *occasion*. Whatever they did in the pit and the gallery those of us fortunate enough to sit in the stalls at the theatre would not have dreamed of doing so in a tweed skirt and cardigan or a suit. It was not snobbery, but a sense of decorum. Also we enjoyed dressing up; it was fun, and if you sat in the stalls it was usual. When we invited friends to dinner we always indicated whether it was a 'black tie' occa-sion or 'informal', and though we joked about 'boiled shirts' they were worn a great deal; and 'tails', of course, for first-nights at the opera or ballet, and for dancing in smart places. There were, too, when tails were worn, those astonishing col-lapsible toppers known as opera hats, as essential an item in the wardrobe of every young man-about-town as the bowler hat, which was generally accepted as the 'only possible head-dress for the well-dressed man', as demonstrated by the attrac-tive and popular Prince of Wales.

I want to end these notes about the theatre and some of the

plays and films that were of interest to us, one way or another, in the Twenties with something intensely nostalgic—a theatre programme of the period. Thanks to my friend Paul Tanqueray, who has a collection of over two thousand theatre programmes, he having been an inveterate theatre-goer since his early youth, there lies beside me as I write the programme of *R.U.R.*, from St. Martin's Theatre, 1923. To begin with, programme was always spelt *programme* in those days before the Americanisation of the language;* and it cost sixpence. The St. Martin's Theatre programme was incorporated with *The ReandeaN Newsheet,* which was 'a complete record of the doings of the ReandeaN Co.'. The Chairman of the ReandeaN Company was Alec Rea, and the Director Basil Dean; hence the name. A considerable cachet attached, always, to a ReandeaN production.

It is interesting to read in the programme that orchestra stalls were twelve shillings, as was the dress circle; the pit, unreserved, was three-and-six. Ladies were 'respectfully asked to add to the comfort of the audience by removing hats and bonnets'. In the advertisement pages there is a notice: 'You cannot buy an ice or a box of chocolates in a theatre after 9.30.' That was the much resented D.O.R.A. (the Defence of the Realm Act) hanging on five years after the end of the War. A whole-page whisky advertisement offers a dozen-case for a hundred and fifty shillings—twelve-and-six a bottle. A restaurant advertises lunch for two-and-three, dinner for two-and-six and three-and-six. A dressmaker describes herself as a 'maker of pretty frocks' and offers 'very moderate terms'. Two pages are devoted to a singularly bad poem, *In a Theatre,* by John Masefield :

> *'Struggling to 's place, a man apologises,*
> *Treading on toes. The safety-curtain rises . . .'*

A piece entitled 'Heard in the Foyer' carries some quite endearingly fatuous jokes: 'Has anybody heard that Karel Capek's first name is Sidney, but that he's left it out in defer-

* *Circa* 1928, with the introduction of the term 'O.K.' from the 'talkies'.

ence to the Sunday Chimes?' A little sketch inset shows a gro-
tesquely dancing couple wearing evening clothes, and the cap-
tion below reads: 'The Robot Roll will be the dance this
season.'

With an eight-page inset of sepia illustrations, and so many
pages of reading matter, *The ReandeaN Newsheet and St.
Martin's Theatre Programme* was a very good six penn'orth
. . . and almost unbearably poignant that advertisement for
whisky at twelve-and-six a bottle.

3

'Hadn't we the gaiety?'

The great aesthetic excitement of the Twenties was undoubtedly the Diaghileff Ballet, but I want to write of this later, in some detail; here I am concerned only to present the general scene.

This Twenties scene was dominated by the dancing craze—the tea-dances and dinner-dances, the night-clubs, and the late-night restaurants with 'floor shows'; the jazz craze, Paul Whiteman's band, the Hammersmith Palais de Danse; Prince's in Piccadilly, the Criterion Roof, Romano's in the Strand, the Savoy—it was very smart to dance at the Savoy after the theatre, between the courses of supper.

You danced whenever and wherever you could; and it was not all Charleston; for one thing that did not reach us from America until 1925, and for another thing, when it did, although we often Charlestoned—it was fun!—very often in the places we frequented there simply was not sufficient floor space for such a kicking up of heels, such a throwing out of legs—for the sheer energetic athleticism of it.

I doubt if we ever Charlestoned at the Ham Bone, that crowded little night-club in Ham Yard, Soho; we were far too densely packed on the pocket handkerchief of a dance floor at the top of the dingy stairs, and to the Ham Bone we would go, we who were young, artistic, unconventional, and, in general, what we liked to call 'Bohemian'. Writers, artists, theatri-

cal people, paid only a guinea-a-year subscription; business
men two or three—as was right and proper.

The Ham Bone was quite chronically 'Bohemian'. In the
bar was a notice: *Work is the curse of the drinking classes.*
This assertion seemed to us not only witty and daring but
somehow to strike a blow for freedom, social and moral. It
cocked a snook at D.O.R.A., and at the Philistines; it was a
gesture of defiance directed at the Establishment—only we
did not know that word then; we referred, simply, to Mrs.
Grundy. We were conscientiously rebels.

Epstein was a member of the Ham Bone Club, and who
more of a rebel than he, whose modernistic sculptures were
always being attacked by the puritans of the Church and
Press? Had anyone suggested that in the course of years the
creator of Rima would accept a title and become Sir Jacob
Epstein we should have hooted with incredulous laughter.

Well, anyhow, so far as I know, Elsie and Doris Waters,
who were also members, never became Dames, nor the Western
Brothers M.B.E. I admired the humour of the Waters sisters
very much; I met them eventually not at the Ham Bone but
at the Café Royal, to discuss a sketch I was to write for them;
they were friendly and nice, and I did some work on the sketch,
but for some reason or other nothing came of it.

Nothing much ever did come of my attempts at plays and
sketches; a sketch for an Archie de Bear revue got no farther
than a try-out at Southampton and was dropped before the
show reached London; a play in which I collaborated with
Frederick Jackson ran for a week at the Theatre Royal, Brighton; it was produced by Leon M. Lion, who himself played
the lead in it. It was called *The Monkey's Tail* and was about
a man with a tail. The rehearsals were hell, with Leon shout-
ing and raving, at me and at the cast. He stormed at me that
he had believed that with my talent I would illuminate the
firmament, but what I had written wouldn't illuminate a drill-
hall. Which was the end of our friendship; a pity, as until then
we had liked and amused each other. He was a great admirer
of Humbert Wolfe and was always giving me copies of his
volumes of poetry, exaggeratedly inscribed. I wrote of him

similarly exaggeratedly in the *Confessions*. But the liking and admiration was genuine at the time, though based on mutual overestimations of brilliance.

I wrote of the Ham Bone in my third novel, *Sounding Brass*, a satire on the advertising world as I had experienced it, published in 1926. I called it the Bacon Rind, and placed it in a mews 'behind Ham Yard'. An entire chapter, entitled 'Jazz', is devoted to it, and 'it was all very noisy and determinedly gay'. A young woman at the Bacon Rind ponders, 'What were they all doing here, all these people, drinking, dancing, philandering, talking, in this hot, overcrowded room that had once been a harness room above a stables? . . . All these short-haired girls sitting about unsentimentally on men's knees, all the cocktails and cigarettes and adventures that made up their lives . . . all things went into their lives, as into a cocktail; their lives were cocktails and they had spiritual indigestion. But didn't they get something out of life, too, something the pre-war youth missed? Their lives were amusing, colourful. But they were hard, these children of the Jazz age; they had Jazz souls. . . .'

Et cetera. But it conveys, nevertheless, something of the 'Jazz Age' scene. It was drawn from life; 1925. The Bacon Rind recurs in another chapter, and the successful advertising man, who has made the mistake of going there in a boiled shirt, clasps the girl with whom he is dancing to his starched bosom and she sings as they shuffle round :

'Oh, it ain't gonna rain no mo', no mo'.'

The novel is a pretty good rant against the vulgarity of the times, but it was fashionable for novelists to rant—Aldous Huxley did it, D. H. Lawrence did it, and they were both writers I greatly admired. The dust-jacket, in black and white, by C. R. W. Nevinson, depicts Piccadilly Circus, with the statue of Eros at the centre, and a confusion of advertisement signs all round; like all Nevinson's work it was considered

wildly modernist. The book has a certain value, I think, as a
portrait of the times; I had forgotten, until I looked at it again,
over forty years later, that we who were young then, and who
kicked up our heels in the Charleston, all but swooned in the
tango, and charged about in one-steps, were still occasionally critical of that very frivolity of which we were a part. It
was a form of self-criticism. There were over two million unemployed by then, and there were hunger marches. With a
part of ourselves we cared, and with another part were in-
different.

The much-criticised youth of today has, I think, vastly more
in the way of social conscience than we 'children of the Jazz
Age', immediately post World War I, ever had.

Yet in spite of the current frivolity of which I was so readily
a part, when I was twenty-five I wrote in *Sounding Brass* of
London, 'suffering from a malaise of unrest, and working it
off in Jazz'. I wrote of a London 'desperately short of homes,
but with no dearth of night-clubs where the new homeless
might forget their problems. A London feverishly extending
its bounds and producing outcrops of inadequate dwellings
destined to be the slums of tomorrow. A London striving to
emulate New York with its electric signs and its palaces of
commerce on the one hand, and Paris, with its cabarets and
dance clubs on the other. . . . A London distraught with a vast
unemployment problem, a housing problem, a traffic problem, a licensing problem; a London in which men upon whom
a few years previously chocolates and cigarettes and endless
socks had been showered, hawking chocolates or playing dis-
mal bands at street corners. A London that had never been
gayer, never more interesting, and never so completely vulgar.'

It seems a little odd, now, to find the 'licensing problem'
included with the housing problem and the unemployment
problem; the reference, I imagine, was to the continuation of
D.O.R.A., which continued to control licensing hours, after
the end of the War. There was certainly a good deal of resentment over it, and it was the subject of bitter cartoons and stage
jokes. But that it should present a 'problem'? And did we

really lavish chocolates as well as socks and cigarettes on the soldiers in World War I? The cigarettes go without saying, and knitting socks for soldiers was part of the female war effort; but choclates? Well, perhaps.

What interests me more is the reminder in my own printed words that the great Exhibition of 1924–5 one always thought of in retrospect simply as 'Wembley', was, in fact, the British Empire Exhibition, and that to it came, from America, the World Advertising Convention. A woman in *Sounding Brass* is told by the advertising man who is what nowadays would be called the anti-hero of the story, that she must come to the sessions of the Convention and learn about advertising as a 'social service', and someone laughs and says that she can't do that because 'she belongs to the W.G.T.W.'s', which, it is explained, is the Won't Go to Wembleys. I had forgotten that some of us had put up a resistance to the Wembley idea as basically imperialist.

In his *Scrapbook for the Twenties* Leslie Baily calls Wembley the 'last shop-window and show-piece of the old Empire', and the 'exuberant super-gimmick of a fading imperialism'.

My own opposition to it was more personal than political, I think, the feeling that it was just not my scene. I put up the same initial resistance decades later to the Festival of Britain, but went in the end, just as I went to the New York World Fair in 1964. That I should eventually go to Wembley was inevitable, since I was married to a man in the advertising world, and the 'Boss', the dynamic Charles Higham, was still around and full of enthusiasm for the Advertising Convention, as might be expected. I don't, really, remember very much about the Exhibition. The Indian Pavilion, a replica of the Taj Mahal, meant something to me because of the poetic description of it in Gilbert Frankau's novel, *Woman of the Horizon*, which Charles Higham had given me, and which had powerfully stirred my youthful imagination; it was to be another twenty-five years before, with my daughter, I was to see it for myself. I remember the floodlighting, which was something new at that time, and the immensity of the great switch-back. I went only the once, and it was enough. Lutyens' fabulous Queen's Doll's House was first shown there, but if I saw it I do not remember; I saw it in recent years, with my little grand-daughter, in Windsor Castle.

It is interesting that in the year in which the great British Empire Exhibition opened at Wembley, Gandhi was in prison in India for civil disobedience as the expression of his opposition to the British Raj, and E. M. Forster's great novel, *A Passage to India*, was published. Another ten years were to pass before I met the man who was to be my second husband, Reginald Reynolds—the man destined to become Gandhi's *Angad*, his messenger, entrusted by him to carry his letter of ultimatum to the Viceroy in 1929, at the height of the Civil Disobedience Campaign. Gandhi's *Angad*, at the time of Wembley, was, at the age of nineteen, a teacher at an *Ecole Normale* in Britanny, where, as he liked to say, the boys all had moustaches and mistresses, whereas he was an unsophisticated and romantic Quaker poet, and, as he wrote in his autobiography,* 'never was such a guileless Daniel thrown to such merciless lions'.

We had two great German films in the second Wembley year, 1925, *Tartuffe* and *Variety*; and we had Charlie Chaplin's *The Gold Rush*. The great Russian film, *Battleship Potemkin*, was made in 1925 but not shown until 1929. The mid-Twenties was the era of silent films; the 'talkies' did not come until 1928, and some of us were opposed for a time to the innovation, insisting that the silent films were more dramatic, just as nowadays some of us go on insisting that black-and-white photography—and this goes for films too—is more dramatic than colour.

We had, too, the excitement of a new star, a Swedish actress called Greta Garbo, about whom we all raved. We had the great D. W. Griffiths 'epics', impressive with great crowd scenes —this, also, was something new—and we had the cartoon character Felix the Cat, who had the vogue that Mickey Mouse was to have much later, but Felix was not a Disney creation; he had his own pleasant silly little song, *Felix kept on walking*.

* *My Life and Crimes*, 1956.

(above) The dining room where so many personalities who were young in the Twenties sat round the table   *(Humphrey and Vera Joel)*

OAK COTTAGE

(below) Beautiful in the spring—and somehow like the White Rabbit's house   *(F. W. Ziemsen)*

(above) left to right: Douglas Goldring, Christina Foyle, Louis Marlow, Violet Hunt

LITERARY LUNCHEON AT OAK COTTAGE, 1929

(below) left to right: Oscar Prescott (Mrs. Charles Spencer), Charles Spencer, and the author, with Richard and Allen Lane

Well, we liked it; we couldn't be highbrow all the time. We had
Charlie Chaplin; he made us laugh, but also it was intellectual
to admire him. It still is.

The supremely highbrow, cultural thing, of course, was the
Diaghileff Ballet, which came to the Alhambra Theatre, London, in 1921, and remained our joy and excitement throughout the Twenties, until its creator died in 1929, and it was the
end of an era as well as of a decade.

4

Going abroad

There were all those intellectual excitements, and there was the 'thrill' of foreign travel—of merely going abroad, but particularly of those daring trips to the Continent by aeroplane. You flew by Imperial Airways, from Croydon Airport; the 'planes were very small—eighteen passengers and a steward —and were also very noisy and bumpy. It was such an adventure that I devoted a whole chapter to it in a book of travel sketches, *All Experience*, published in 1932, and nearly forty years later it makes completely fascinating reading, like a message from Mars. It is all very knowledgeable and informative. The presumably inexperienced reader is warned that those who suffer from seasickness are liable to suffer from airsickness, but that the 'airline companies thoughtfully provide each passenger with an aluminium cuspidor—cardboard cartons on German 'planes and paper bags in the French machines'. There was only one row of seats aside in those 'planes, with a narrow gangway between, so that no privacy was possible in the event of airsickness, though it was worse, apparently, in the 'new super-Hannibal machines', because then you had a passenger facing you. However, in the 'new de luxe machines' there was lavatory accommodation, and in the 'big new airliners' the noise was considerably minimised, 'sufficiently so, indeed, as to obviate the necessity for plugging the ears with cotton wool'.

It is interesting to be reminded that at that time 'women were still very much in the minority as air passengers, particularly on the longer journeys', and that 'flying to Amsterdam and Frankfurt I have been the only woman passenger on each occasion'—as I was, it seems, when a Paris 'plane came down at Lympne, 'unable to finish the journey because of fog over the Channel, with the result that we were all sent down to the coast by car to pick up the boat we would have caught had we gone by the eleven o'clock train from Victoria. But as a philosophic Dutch business man pointed out to me, as we crouched round the stove in a bleak wooden hut at Lympne awaiting the pilot's verdict on wireless reports as to conditions over the Channel, it is what we English call "all experience".'

On another occasion, on a flight to Frankfurt, 'the sun was shining when we left Croydon, but before we reached the coast we ran into rain, and flew so low that we terrified chickens, horses, cattle, who fled in all directions as the 'plane passed over. However, we reached Brussels safely and came down long enough for refreshments. I had a coffee and cigarette with the pilot at the aerodrome café; he asked me if I was on the stage, and I asked him if we should make the journey.'

At Cologne, the narrative continues, there was an hour to wait for the Frankfurt 'plane, and I had lunch with the pilot, and we drank beer and had a discussion on marriage, love, freedom. He was, it is recorded, 'very charming and intelligent'.

Undoubtedly those were the days! Since then I have flown from the vast impersonality of London Airport to New York, Washington, Tokyo, Rangoon, not to mention the nearer places such as Baghdad, Beirut, Amman, Cairo, with nothing to report but boredom.

But in those days it was not only the journeying that was exciting, whether done in a flying machine or more conventionally by boat and train; it was 'thrilling' merely to arrive in a foreign place—to be 'abroad'. We loved to write letters and postcards home, from the South of France and Italy, exclaiming lyrically about the sun—especially if we were writing home in January—and the blueness of the sea, roses in bloom, the scent of mimosa, the gaiety and colour of life in foreign parts

—with an implication of the contrasting greyness and drab-
ness of the life we had left behind; there was a certain pitying
condescension in it all, a what-do-they-know-of-living-who-
only-England-know. We loved to write sitting at pavement
cafés, to show how assimilated we had become into life abroad;
words like *bistro, demi-bière, vin ordinaire,* were precious to
us—'I write this sitting at our favourite *bistro,* sipping a *demi-
bière . . .*' That would be from Paris; from the South the sun,
the sea, the mimosa, the bougainvillaea, would be more important, because back in old England it would be raining, for
sure, and cold, and grey, and the trees bare as skeletons. In
Italy we really let ourselves go; a flower-seller offering sprays
of almond blossom at the bottom of the Spanish Steps in Rome
sent us into ecstasies—you would think we had invented both
almond blossom and the Spanish Steps. What I wrote about
Rome in *All Experience,* in 1931, turns me now, in 1970, side-
ways with distaste. Yet . . . I did love Rome, and it's all there,
under the brashness and rashness and showing-off. I loved
Rome as I have only, since, loved Jerusalem . . . before the
Occupation.

Nowadays, when 'everyone' does just naturally go abroad
for their spring or summer holidays, or both, to the Costa
Brava or Majorca—fully equipped now, I understand, with
fish-and-chip shops—or whatever is the package attraction,
flying there and back, and everything pre-paid and pre-
arranged, there is something delightfully old-world and
'period' to come upon a whole chapter, in this book of travel
sketches, on 'Going Abroad', urging that Victoria Station is
'one of the most romantic places in the world—certainly the
most romantic in England', because it is the Gateway to the
Continent, which is the Gateway to Adventure, and urging,
along with this, that 'going abroad' is the most exciting and
romantic phrase in the language :

'Going abroad . . . coming into a foreign city, a foreign port;
getting out at the Gare du Nord and smelling that combination of coffee and garlic and French cigarettes and drains
which is forever Paris—one of the best smells in life; or waking
up in the morning after a night crossing and seeing the pro-

mised land through the porthole, a rock coastline, or tall houses
with the bloom of strangeness on them; or going South overnight, leaving Paris at six in the evening, and at six in the morning tearing through Arles and Avignon and getting one's first
glimpse of cypresses and olive trees and vineyards, that first
ecstatic savouring of the South. . . .'

Et cetera, et cetera, et cetera.

All the same it was exciting. Which being processed from
a 'plane at some international airport can hardly be said to be.

In common with many writers and artists of my generation
I had a period of living a good deal abroad in the early Thirties,
as I have recorded in *Privileged Spectator*; it was the 'Bohemian' thing to do, and we followed each other around, in Paris
at the Dôme, the Select, the Flore, and in the cheap restaurants of Montparnasse and St. Germain de Près; we went south
and encountered each other again in the sailors' bars and cafés
of Toulon and Villefranche. At Villefranche we patronised
the Welcome Hotel because Jean Cocteau had once stayed
there; there was a Polish bar in Vienna we 'all' frequented,
and a *fonda*, a muleteers' tavern, outside Palma, in Majorca.
But it had all begun in the Twenties, as Douglas Goldring
records in his book, in which he declares that 'one of the circumstances which enhanced the rapture of being alive in the
Twenties and young enough to enjoy oneself was the opportunity created by the high value of sterling of going abroad. Life
was cheaper almost everywhere in Europe than it was in England, and in congested Paris . . . an English pound went three
times as far as it did in London', where 'drinks were dear, pubs
opened late and closed early, and financial depression soon
followed on the post-war boom'. So painters and free-lance
writers crossed the Channel to sunnier climates where the
drinks were cheaper.

My own visits to the Continent in the Twenties, however,
were of a different order, a series of forays undertaken in the
spirit of adventure and what was then called *joie de vivre*. I
went abroad because only the most unimaginative bourgeois
would not have done so when opportunity offered, and I was
bursting with imagination and very far removed from bour-

geois. I recorded in *All Experience* : 'When I was twenty-three, with one suit-case, a portable typewriter, a child of three, and six words of French, I realised the dream which had been burning in me since I was twelve, and went South, in search of the sun, violet fields, olive groves, and orange trees.'

> '*I'd always wanted for to see*
> *An orange growing on a tree.*'

I wanted palm trees, too, because they were somehow the essence of 'abroad', and I chose Hyères because according to a travel brochure it was Hyères-les-Palmiers, and an illustration depicted a palm avenue, and palm trees were the essence of foreignness—of 'abroad'. I stayed in a pension with a balcony overlooking the Toulon road, and I enjoyed it all hugely, the steep cobbled streets of the old town, the thyme-covered hills behind, the avenues of palm trees, the violet fields, the orange and olive groves, the mimosa, cypress, bougainvillaea—the lot; and in due course wrote of it all, lyrically, in a chapter on Provence.

Sea cruises began to be fashionable in the Twenties, and with my husband I went on a cruise from Liverpool in one of the Fyffe banana boats, to Lisbon, the Canary Islands, Madeira —where in the market-place at Funchal I took a photograph which was used on the dust-cover of *All Experience*; it was rather a good picture, of a cobbled square with a man drinking at a fountain overhung by a tree. With my husband, also, I journeyed, by ship and train, to Brussels, Bruges, Ghent; in Brussels I was daringly photographed beside the *mannikin pis* fountain, and bought postcards of the peeing little boy to send home to scandalise untravelled friends. I reacted romantically to the famous thirteenth-century belfry in Bruges, and it all found its way into my fourth novel, *Pilgrims*, set in Amsterdam, Flanders, Paris, and published early in 1927, with a futuristic dust-cover by E. McKnight Kauffer—very *avant-garde*. To Amsterdam and The Hague I had travelled, as to Hyères, with a small child in one hand and a portable typewriter in the other, but the child was five by then; and in this fashion, also, I journeyed all along the coast, from Toulon, spending some time in Monte Carlo, then across the border to Rapallo—my first incursion into Italy.

At Rapallo, on the way to Rome, I encountered Osbert Sitwell in a café, and he very kindly invited me to lunch, with the child, at the cottage he had rented at the side of the mule-track that climbs the hillside behind the town—or did; more than forty years later a motor road may have replaced the mule-track, or the hillside become plastered with villas. I had met Osbert Sitwell previously at a literary party in London and had no idea he was in Rapallo. I wrote about all this in an impertinent chapter in my *Confessions*; years later, I am glad to say, I wrote to Mr. Sitwell—as he was then—deploring my youthful ill-manners and asking his forgiveness, which he was gracious enough to give in the most generous terms, writing me that my letter had made him very happy, and that I should 'never think of it again', adding that there were 'too many packs of wolves out these days' for us to quarrel—that one could only *enjoy* rows when there was 'less real misery in the world'.

The truth was that I met too many people in the Twenties, before I was mature enough to form any valid assessments or appreciations of such diverse—and in some cases distinguished—personalities. I had too much too soon, like many of us; too much facile success, too much money, too much unassimilated experience, and whilst it was *fun* to be young in the Twenties, and exciting, it was also a *bad* time in which to be young, because for all the surface gaiety it was a decade of social and moral decay.

But from the literary point of view nothing was 'wasted' in all this traipsing round Europe; all was grist to the mill, and Rapallo and Rome got into *Crescendo*, my sixth novel, published in January, 1929. It was a novel which meant a good deal to me at the time, but it was brash and rash, and ultimately melodramatic. It followed a quiet novel about childhood, *Green Willow*, written whilst living in a house which looked into a weeping willow, and which I came to think of as the house of the willow tree, and the novel, published in

1928, was inspired by it and centred round it.

By then I had made my first visit to New York, going over for the American publication of *Sounding Brass*, and travelling with a woman friend who edited a woman's magazine for which I wrote romantic-sentimental love-stories. As travelling companions we were not really suited, for she was staid whilst I was flighty, and as rigidly conventional as I was recklessly 'Bohemian', which was trying for us both, though we were still friends when we got back to Southampton some weeks later.

New York City during Prohibition was no place for the irresponsible young person I was then, for it abounded in 'speak-easies', which sprang up everywhere to provide the forbidden liquor—and much of it was wood alcohol. Outwitting Prohibition was a very popular pastime, and for those who felt strongly enough about it assumed the proportions of a moral and social duty. It was the done thing to carry a hip flask containing spirits to add to the mineral waters in restaurants, and the waiters turned a blind eye. It was all crazy; there were places in which cocktails were served in soup cups in the belief that if the cops raided the place they would be fooled. Because it was illegal everyone who liked to drink and who could afford the bootleg prices drank like mad.

At the time, of course, it all seemed the wildest fun, and I wrote about it all, exuberantly, in the *Confessions*. New York, I declared, was 'an adventure in freedom'. But it did not produce a novel; the novel I wrote when I got back from America —more precisely from Canada, for an artist friend had driven us up from New York to Montreal and on to Quebec, from which we sailed—was the one with the European background, *Pilgrims*. Something of the brief Canadian experience got into *Crescendo*, but New York itself had to wait for the *Confessions*, some three years later, and by that time I had left my husband and the house of the willow tree, opting for independence and freedom, not compatible with the married state; that such opting-out was both selfish and irresponsible did not for a moment occur to me, for I was eight-and-twenty, intensely of my period, and it was a period in which freedom was all.

The author at
Hyères-les-Palmiers,
1924

Dr. Norman Haire
at Oak Cottage, with
open-necked shirt,
sandals, knicker-
bockers, altogether
Dress Reform . . .
1934

(*above*) The blue and orange 'dance room' with bar

THE HOUSE OF THE WILLOW TREE

(*below*) The other end of the 'dance room' with blue and orange wind-up gramophone, 1925

5

Coming down whole water

The years 1926–9 have been described as the 'heyday of the
Bright Young Things', though I am inclined to agree with
Douglas Goldring that the early Thirties, the immediate post-
war years, were the really 'marvellous'—to use his word—
years, when, as he says, the 'younger artists and intellectuals
. . . had their uninhibited fling'. They were marvellous because
freedom, then, was still a novelty, and heady. By the middle
of the decade some of the grim realities began to impinge on
the fun; some of the muddy water of the rising tide of misery
and despair in the industrial north, where mass unemployment
made a bitter mockery of the jubilant war-time promise of a
'land fit for heroes to live in' when it was all over, began to
seep through to the south. By May, 1926, the tide could no
longer be contained, and there was the General Strike. For
years we had been singing, as we cavorted round the floor at
the tea-dances, the dinner-dances, the supper-dances, the
night-clubs, '*It ain't gonna rain no mo*', *no mo*', *it ain't gonna
rain no mo*' ', but now it was raining hard; pelting; coming
down whole water. Even in London we knew it; the General
Strike caused a good deal of inconvenience. . . .

It was in 1928 that George Orwell, newly returned from
Burma, was so shocked by the moral degradation of mass unemployment; and in 1929 was the year of the slump that followed the Wall Street crash. With all that the hedonistic young

person I was then was not greatly concerned; for me 1926 was the year I first went to America; it was the year I changed my hair-style to the severe centre parting one by which I was to become known, through all the press pictures, and from which I have never changed. As we should say nowadays, I created that particular 'image' of myself. I was inspired to it by the *corps de ballet,* in which all the lovely creatures wore their hair in this plain, smooth fashion; why did I not do likewise, I asked myself, disliking going to the hairdressers to be 'waved' as intensely as I did. I was not attracted to the fashionable 'shingle' or 'Eton crop', the one too feminine, the other too masculine, it seemed to me; besides, I liked having long hair; all I wanted was to have done with the tedium of hairdressers, and this 'ballet style' suddenly seemed to me the answer. I tried it out and liked what I saw in the mirror.

The innovation caused a certain amount of protest among family and friends; my poor mother was quite upset— 'making yourself look like a washerwoman', she called it. Only at A. S. Neill's school, where tastes were artistic and ideas unorthodox, was there approval. But nothing would have stopped me; this was how the *corps de ballet* wore it, and so would I.

James Laver, in his book *Between the Wars,** says that in the Twenties women cut off their hair so that they could wear the fashionable cloche hats; some may have done so for that reason; my own view is that most did so in order to be in the current fashion, and long hair did not prevent me from wearing cloche hats galore—and other, more remarkable, forms of millinery.

In sociological terms, it had already begun to rain hard in 1925; it was the year of hunger-marches and misery, hopelessness and resentment, and by the spring of 1926 the gathering storm broke and there was the deluge of the General Strike. Despite my preoccupation with my impending American trip I was still sufficiently socialistic at heart to feel indignation against the uprush of middle-class patriotism opposing the strikers, with undergraduates rushing to man the buses, and

* 1961.

bitterness against the T.U.C. leaders when, after nine days of what seemed like near-revolution, the strike collapsed and the workers went back on the bosses' terms—everyone but the miners, whose struggle it was, and who, after their betrayal, stayed out for six months in a steadily mounting misery. My political detestation of Winston Churchill dates from that time; he edited the Government emergency news-sheet, the *British Gazette*, and was all for bringing out the troops against the strikers.

Nineteen-twenty-nine was the year of the General Election which returned Labour to power again, but for me it was the year I opted for independence. In June I moved into Oak Cottage, the 'dream house' I had wanted since I was about five years old, and which, when I was ready for a house of my own, was available—a fact I have never ceased to regard as astonishing—and where now, in June, 1970, I write this. In that first summer of independence I finished *Children of the Earth*, a novel about Jersey fisherfolk, published the following year, and worked on the *Confessions*, the work with which I ended the decade. The storm clouds were gathering for me, too, though I didn't know it.

On my twenty-ninth birthday I gave a dinner party in the upstairs room at the Ivy Restaurant, to which we 'all' went in those years—writers, theatrical people, publishers. I announced it in the invitation as a 'farewell to the Twenties' party, but it was to my own Twenties I was bidding adieu, not the decade drawing to a close in a sociological and economic deluge. What I thought or felt or did on New Year's Eve I have no idea; I was never one for New Year Eves; so far as I am concerned January 1 is always just another day.

That, then, was the general 'scene' of what has been variously called the Amoral Decade, the Sweet and Twenties, the Bitter-Sweet Twenties, the Gay Twenties, the Bright Twenties, the Roaring Twenties, but which is perhaps best described by Leslie Baily as 'this extremely mixed-up decade', and the 'age of ambivalence'.

PART II

Enfant du siècle

6

Puritans in our midst

The American author, Vincent Sheehan, who is of my own
generation, writing in 1932, in his fine book *In Search of History*, declares: 'My testimony, for what it is worth, would be
that my generation had practically no moral sense as that term
had been hitherto understood,' adding that 'this is not a judgment; I am in this, as in other respects, an *enfant du siècle*,
and have no right or desire to judge anybody's morals; but if
we adopt the point of view of history we must see that these
phenomena constitute decay from what preceded. We may
like it or not (I like it, at least in preference to bourgeois re-
spectability); but the fact is that people who were in their
Twenties in the 1920's were amazingly, perhaps unprece-
dentedly, immoral.'

This immorality he catalogues as promiscuity, homosexuality, 'unlimited indulgence in strong drink, and, often enough
in drugs'. Nor was all this, he points out, confined to the 'Bohemians' of London and the Paris Left Bank, but was rampant
among young people of the respectable middle-class, and
though he does not use the term 'generation gap', it being not
then in vogue, he speaks of the immense gulf between the
younger generation and their parents so that 'frank conversation' was impossible. It reads rather like an indictment of the
present-day younger generation, except that they have a social
conscience which we who were young in the Twenties singularly

lacked. Our sexual emancipation was an exciting novelty to us, a splendid feature of the brave new world of the post-war era, and we were preoccupied with it, almost besotted with it, but for all that we were not as free as the young of to-day, for we had not quite sloughed off some of the sentimental-romantic trappings of the past. Perhaps it would be truer to say that we were amoral rather than immoral. There was a sense in which our sophistication was only skin deep. We had a certain naïveté; in all seriousness we talked about the Art of Living, and Living Life to the Full, spelling it out in maju-scules, and a man could call a woman, 'You lovely thing!' in the full flush of ardour and she would be 'thrilled'. Used in that context the word, viewed from the Seventies, has a curiously old-world flavour, like 'sex-appeal', and having 'It'.

It was Elinor Glyn, the great romance-fiction novelist of the period, who invented 'It' for sexual attraction. 'It' was something every female young thing reckoned to have. *Three Weeks* was perhaps the most famous of the Elinor Glyn stories of daring romantic passion—'daring' because nearly explicit —and a rhyme was current at the time:

> '*Would you like to sin*
> *On a tiger-skin,*
> *With Elinor Glyn?*
> *Or would you prefer*
> *To err*
> *On another fur?*'

I never read *Three Weeks,* nor saw the film made of it in 1924, and which was considered sensational because of a pas-sionate scene on a tiger-skin-covered couch; all that celluloid sexiness was not for us who were so intensively—you might almost say dedicatedly—busy with the Real Thing. 'Sex-appeal' was a phrase we used a good deal, and those of us who had it—who had 'It'—exploited it to the full, determinedly outraging 'Mrs. Grundy' . . . has anyone even heard of her nowadays? She died, probably, during World War II.

In spite of the 'unprecedented' immorality, the nineteen-twenties was not a 'permissive' decade; for all the gin-and-sin there were not the extremes of licence which obtain today; practising homosexuals could be and sometimes were sent to prison. Radclyffe Hall's entirely decent novel of homosexual female love, *The Well of Loneliness*, was banned in 1928, and James Joyce's *Ulysses* was touted round the Left Bank cafés in Paris and your copy was seized by the Customs at Dover if you were not careful. We all read the last chapter, Mollie Bloom's soliloquy, and it was fashionable to assert that no one but the author had ever read the rest; but to have read that last chapter was almost required reading for anyone with any pretensions to modernity—and we were as madly modern as our hideous chromium-plated furniture and strident 'Jazz Age' décor.

We all, of course, passionately defended the banned books, *Ulysses*, the *Well*, *Lady Chatterley*—and there were others—regardless of their literary merit. I have forgotten, now, in what circumstances I met Radclyffe Hall and her friend and companion, Una Troubridge; perhaps I wrote to Radclyffe Hall when the *Well* was prosecuted—very many people did write to her—but anyhow she and Lady Troubridge came here, and I later visited them both at their seventeenth-century cottage at Rye. I wrote with great admiration of Radclyffe Hall in *Confessions*, and in 1962, writing from Rome, where she was living, Una Troubridge sent me a copy of her biography, *The Life and Death of Radclyffe Hall*, published in 1961. She wrote to me because she had been reading my novel, *Curfew at Dawn*, about a young man who became blind and deaf, published that year. She wanted, she wrote, to express her 'very great admiration of its originality and treatment'; she sent me, with the letter, what she called her '*one* book, apart from translations', because 'you knew John* and have written your appreciation of her and of her work'. On the title page of the book she wrote: 'For Ethel Mannin, who knew John and has written of her in words that moved me deeply, and has written of animals in words that moved *her* deeply. In friendship, I hope . . .' I was touched because we

* The name by which Radclyffe Hall elected to be known.

had not kept in touch in the intervening thirty years; she died
shortly afterwards, twenty years after her beloved John's death
from cancer in 1943. Her account of Radclyffe Hall's dreadful
illness and death is very moving; Radclyffe Hall was a woman
of tremendous courage, moral and physical. She faced life and
death equally bravely.

In her book Una Troubridge describes Radclyffe Hall in
her youth as 'like a handsome young man'; when I met her in
1928 she would have been, I suppose, in her early forties, and
she was still very handsome, with her thick slightly waving
fair hair swept back from a high forehead, her finely shaped
head, and her high cheekbones. As I wrote of her at the time,
I thought her one of the handsomest women I had ever met,
masculine, but attractively so. I had remembered her as very
serious in her expression and manner, and had forgotten the
'charming boyish smile' which could suddenly light up the
pale grave face with its slight suggestion of severity. But I have
remembered her as somewhat humourless, though I did not
record it, being so passionately on her side against the puritans. Una Troubridge, who was feminine, I found easier—
warmer, more relaxed, and it surprised me that it was she who
wore the monocle. She, too, was very good-looking, and wore
her hair short, but not cropped like Radclyffe's. She, too, I
think, had considerable courage, enabling her to face the anguish of that last year of their long and devoted relationship
with fortitude. They were both sustained by their Roman
Catholic faith, and I think it worth recording that when in the
course of that last correspondence I asked her how they
squared their religion with their relationship, what they did
about Confession, she replied to me, simply, 'There was nothing to confess.' She was old, then, and near to her own death,
and I see no reason to disbelieve that statement.

Ironically, after the *Well* had been suppressed here it was reprinted in Paris, was translated into eleven languages, and sold
a million copies in America. Fourteen years after publication
here, Una Troubridge reports, the *Well* had a 'steady annual
sale of over one hundred thousand copies' in America, despite

the efforts of the American opposite number of our own prize
puritan, James Douglas, to get it suppressed. James Douglas
was a journalist who ranted from the columns of the *Sunday
Express* that he would 'rather give a healthy boy or girl a phial
of prussic acid than *The Well of Loneliness* to read'.

The young author who was myself he attacked as one of the
'novelists who go too far', though what he can have had in
mind it is difficult to say, as I had written no 'obscene' novel,
and up to that time had not even published the *Confessions*.
Perhaps it was because I wrote 'immoral' articles championing
what were then called 'companionate marriages 'or 'trial marriages'.

We had a plague of puritans in England at that time. We
had an aggressively puritanical Home Secretary, Sir William
Joynson-Hicks, commonly known as Jix, who was anti alcohol,
night-clubs, gambling, the poems and paintings of D. H.
Lawrence, 'obscene' books, and all things 'sinful'. We had,
too, as though James Douglas was not enough, another journalist fanatic called Hannen Swaffer, who was not only anti
homosexuals but anti Negroes, and who was worried about
Paul Robeson playing Othello because Desdemona would be
a white woman—she was, in fact, to be—in 1930—the young
and lovely Peggy Ashcroft. After I had met Swaffer I wrote
about him in *Confessions* as a 'portrait of a puritan'. I reported
with satisfaction that an American actress had walked into the
Savoy Grill, where he used to lunch, and smacked his face, and
that he wrote an article in a Sunday newspaper the following
Sunday entitled 'He Who Gets Slapped'—to 'save his face',
I said, I think unconsciously punning. In retrospect it seems
to me that he did so was one up to him.

We had these and other puritans in our midst, and as an
emancipated, rebellious, and Angry Young Woman I wrote
that puritanism was 'rapidly making this country no fit place
for a decent, intelligent person to live in'—a somewhat extreme statement in view of the general moral laxity. The puritans could shout their heads off, and did, but we who were
young were the post-war generation, the 'children of the Jazz
Age', and the voices we listened to urged us away from the

pre-war taboos and inhibitions; they were the voices of Freud, D. H. Lawrence, Aldous Huxley, Dr. Marie Stopes, Bertrand Russell. Free-love, trial marriages, birth-control, these were our slogans, in a sense our battle-cries as we surged forward under the glorious banner of sexual emancipation. We confused freedom with licence, of course, but the gain was greater than the loss. The emancipation of women was a big thing, important to women of all social classes and all degrees of intelligence. The new attitude to love and sex, marriage and divorce, and the dissemination of knowledge about contraception and the setting up of birth-control clinics to which women could go for advice and to be fitted with contraceptives, was a liberation both physical and spiritual. Women discovered that for them, too, the 'weaker sex', the 'second sex', life was made for living. It was a dangerous discovery, with contraception offering a challenge to chastity—'love without fear'—and freedom in terms of 'free love' opposing marriage. It was a moral revolution, nothing less, and therefore destructive of the traditional conventions of premarital chastity, and even of married love itself.

It was an exciting time in which to be young; it was a decade of uninhibited living—relatively. In a sense it was an Age of Innocence, in which foreign travel was an adventure, and falling in love, no matter how ephemerally, endowed with romantic passion. The young people of today are more honest in their sexual relations—more honest with themselves and with each other—in their refusal to sentimentalise and romanticise their promiscuity, but it does reduce things, somewhat, to the farmyard level of the 'cock that treads the hen—and flaps un's wings and treads agen'.

The 1920's was a decade of paradoxes, of surface gaiety and hidden misery, of a generation dedicated to the pursuit of happiness in terms of sex freedom, and to good times in terms of cocktail parties, dancing, night life, but all of it a gaudy superstructure imposed on the black, rotting foundation of the economic depression. London was one thing; industrial England another. It was two nations; two worlds. In London the theatres boomed with spectacular musicals and revues, the night-clubs were packed (at the Florida you danced on a glass floor lit from underneath, at Ciro's you might see the Prince of Wales), and there were 'wild parties' galore for the Bright Young Things, the Mayfair socialites. Of what it was like in the grey wilderness outside that glittering oasis George Orwell wrote, in shock and anger, in *The Road to Wigan Pier.** In his *Scrapbook for the Twenties* Leslie Baily observed: 'The West End in 1928 had no apparent connection with that other half of the nation that queued for doles rather than stalls.'

Douglas Goldring, in *The Nineteen Twenties*, writing of some successful novelists of the decade—Alec Waugh, Gilbert Frankau, G. B. Stern, Sheila Kaye-Smith, Michael Arlen, Margaret Kennedy—mentions 'a notable newcomer, Ethel Mannin, who later in her career developed a social conscience, fortunately without diminishing her sales'. The social conscience of that barbed remark had, I regret to say, to wait for the Thirties; in the Twenties it got buried under the rubble of the 'good times' which, as Aldous Huxley observed, early on, were 'chronic' with us. And not only the good times, but the ease with which, if you were young and bright, and possessed of a journalistic flair, as I was, money could be made. In the second half of the decade, I had money to burn for the first time in my life, and I burnt it—if not on riotous living anyhow on frivolous living, on clothes and parties and extravagances; all the early socialism went under, and the social conscience was nowhere in sight.

That with a part of myself I was aware that the gaiety was pretty shallow and trashy is evidenced by the tirades against the 'Jazz Age' that appeared in some of those early novels—as in *Sounding Brass*—but they were the 'dancing years' and I danced them, *enfant du siècle*, in love with life, with love, with freedom, with the whole heady business of being young in the Twenties.

* 1937.

7

Nothing if not progressive

It was not all frivolity and freedom-run-wild, however; there were intellectual excitements as well; there was a new translation of Freud's *Introductory Lectures in Psychoanalysis*, published here in 1922 with an introduction by Ernest Jones; there were the new ideas in education expounded by A. S. Neill in his book, *The Problem Child*, brought out again in 1925, the first edition in 1915 having been a war-time casualty. The impact of Freud and A. S. Neill on the young intelligentsia of the Twenties was profound. The excitement over Freud's interpretation of dreams and analysis of neuroses led on naturally to an eager, excited response to Neill's Freudian approach to child psychology and his revolutionary ideas on education stemming from that.

I have told in the *Confessions*, in the chapter on A. S. Neill, how I first learned about him and his 'free' school whilst crossing on the night boat to Dieppe with two art students with whom I was going to Paris to gather material for my novel, *Pilgrims*. The students, a young married couple, asked me about my child and told me what they would do with theirs, if they had one, which, I gathered, was not bring it up but leave it to grow up, and instead of having it 'messed about' by orthodox education would send it to Neill's school, where the kids were free to attend lessons or not, as they pleased. Neill had started the school in Germany, before the war, they said, and now it was at Lyme Regis, and his wonderful book, *The Problem Child,* had just been republished here. They explained that Neill had begun his career as a conventional schoolmaster in Scotland, but had eventually been thrown out of Scottish educational circles for his unorthodox ideas, particularly for his attacks on Calvinism, and he had written *A Dominie's Log,* and a *Dominie in Doubt,* and finally *A Dominie Dismissed*; surely I knew? I didn't know, but was eager to learn. I had doubts about the value of orthodox education myself, and it seemed most wonderful that there existed someone who had the courage and the ability to put such ideas into practice.

When I got back to London I bought a copy of *The Problem Child,* and was so excited that I wrote to Neill, and soon afterwards, at his invitation, went to see him at Lyme Regis. I discovered, of course, that though I hadn't known about his pioneering educational work he had an international reputation. I discovered, too, that the new ideas about education were in the air; Bertrand Russell ran a school, not as 'free' as Neill's, but on unorthodox lines; and there were others. It was all part of the new post-war freedom; it was 1925, and I was not yet twenty-five, and fertile ground for new ideas—in education and child psychology as in all else. I wrote about Neill's school in the 1928 novel, *Green Willow,* but did not write *Commonsense and the Child,* for which he wrote the preface, until 1930. When I went to America in 1926 I sent my daughter, not yet six years old, to Neill's school; I think now that it is much too young to send a child away to school, but I was young-and-twenty, driven by youthful egotism and powerfully under the influence of the new ideas in all directions. It is a characteristic of youth, not confined to that decade, that whatever is new is necessarily progressive and therefore an improvement on the old, and in the 1920's we were nothing if not 'progressive'.

Neill had only some half dozen or so pupils at that time, but his personality and ideas, and the atmosphere at the school, opened up a new world for me; it was a world in which freedom was not merely an idea but, quite simply, a way of life. It was totally, but unself-consciously, unconventional; I wrote enthusiastically in the *Confessions*, in an attempt to convey this, 'You feel that if you turned up to lunch in a loin-cloth nobody would take much notice . . . Perhaps it all sounds a little "mad", and coming from the artificiality of the outer world it seems so at first, but how refreshing it all is after everybody else's smothering "sanity".'

I enjoyed, too, the internationalism of the atmosphere, the variety of nationalities both amongst the staff and the children, and the presence of Germans and Swedes somehow added to the feeling of progressiveness—Germany and Sweden were associated with *avant-garde* ideas, particularly with regard to education. The school, Summerhill, was in the big old house at the top of the steep hill that climbs up from Lyme Regis quay—the school has been now for very many years in Leiston, Suffolk, but it is still called Summerhill. I always enjoyed visiting that first Summerhill, staying in a cottage overlooking the sea and going up in the mornings to the school. I had a tremendous liking and admiration for Neill's partner, an attractive, intelligent and vital Australian woman, Mrs. Lindesay-Neustatter, always known as 'Mrs. Lins', and who in 1927 became the first Mrs. Neill—a fact of which parents were notified in some end-of-term notes, 'p.s. Neill and Mrs. Lins have married'. I wrote of her as the 'sanest and most lovable woman I had ever met', and a 'lovely person'—the expression is dated, but not the quality it conveys. When she died, in April, 1944, I had somewhat lost touch with the school, though not with Neill, and it was impossible not to feel that stricken sense of something irreplaceable having been extinguished at Summerhill; it was difficult even after about twenty years to think of Summerhill without 'Mrs. Lins'. She had that quality of warmth and vitality combined with forthrightness and no-nonsense I have always liked in women, and which in my experience is more often met with in women than in men.

Neill dedicated the book he was working on in the year of her death to her, 'To "Mrs. Lins" '. The book was entitled, *Hearts Not Heads in the School*, and was published in 1945; he devotes the last chapter to 'Mrs. Lins' and pays a fine tri-

bute to her, declaring that without her help he doubts whether
Summerhill would have survived its early struggles. 'Her courage was tremendous,' he writes, 'and she had a natural, often
brilliant, understanding of child psychology which made her
an ideal partner in the work.' The school had to evacuate to
Wales during the Second World War and she was unhappy
about it and began to go downhill; in that last illness she suffered much, Neill records, at the realisation that she could no
longer work, and her life became weary and empty.

But it was a fine, vigorous and unselfish life, and as Neill
says, 'Her memorial will lie in the lives of many boys and girls
and adults who were helped by her, encouraged by her, loved
by her. She left the world just a little richer, because she tried
to do something new and important . . . Her epitaph might
well be: "She belonged to tomorrow, to youth, to hope." '

Bertrand Russell I did not meet until some years later. Because his school was not as extreme in its freedom as A. S.
Neill's I was not much interested in it. I admired his views
concerning love, sex, marriage, and cherished in 1928 a little
book of his essays entitled, *What I Believe*, first published in
1925. I find that in the essay on Moral Rules I marked a passage: 'If we were right in saying that the good life is inspired
by love and guided by knowledge, it is clear that the moral
code of any community is not ultimate and self-sufficient, but
must be examined with a view to seeing whether it is such as
wisdom and benevolence would have decreed.' More than
forty years later there seems nothing wrong with that, though
it is not, I think, anything I would have been moved to mark
now. I admired his *Sceptical Essays*, 1928, and I find that his
Marriage and Morals, the American edition of which, published in 1929, he gave to me, inscribed, in February, 1930, is
full of markings, mostly in connection with assertions concerning 'the taboo on sex knowledge', though in the chapter
on divorce I have both marked and underlined the assertion
that 'the psychology of adultery has been falsified by conventional morals'.

I have forgotten, now, the circumstances in which I met
him, but according to my *Confessions* we had an enormous

conversation on a wide range of subjects one afternoon in 'the tower' in which he worked; where this 'tower' was is not specified, but it is described as 'book-lined' and with windows facing in all directions; as I was never at the Petersfield house he had then, and he had a flat in London, I imagine this 'tower' was there. I had at that time, anyhow, a tremendous admiration for him, and wrote about him, in the most extravagant terms, as the 'greatest living intellect of our age'. I quoted, proudly, the compliment he paid me of saying that talking with me was more exciting than making love with almost anyone else—which, of course, was nonsense, for intellectual excitement is one thing and sexual excitement another, but the young woman with so much 'It' naturally enjoyed the compliment paid to her intellect by the great intellectual. The 'almost' was inserted at his request; there was a lady in America, he wrote me, after receiving the typescript of my piece about him, who would be 'pained and angry' if she read what I had written, and this he would regret; 'her talk also is exciting, less so than yours, but it would be rude to say so in print'. Did I mind? I expect I did; anyhow I inserted the qualifying almost. He wrote me that I overestimated him, but that it was 'very delicious' to be so overestimated—he was fond of that somewhat confectionery word—and that what I had written, though it had made him blush, had been 'quite a considerable event' to him. Only from a preface by Einstein to a German translation of one of his books had he had 'such strong delight from praise', he declared. The praise had made him think better of himself, to which he adds, rather oddly, 'For I do not think you are much in love with me.' I was in fact not in the least in love with him. I found him physically unattractive, and thought him very old—he was at that time fifty-eight, which was twenty-eight years older than I was. His attraction for me was purely, as I wrote of him, as a 'first-class mind'.

In later years I came to think less highly of him—perhaps under the influence of Reginald Reynolds, who visited him at his country house in the Thirties and found him 'disappointing'. They talked of Gandhi, not at Reginald's wish, 'but because Russell kept returning to the subject'. Had they discussed passive resistance, pacifism, or the political situation in India with reference to Gandhi, Reginald wrote,* 'the conversation might still have had some value; but Bertrand Russell only seemed to be interested in one thing about Gandhi, which was that Gandhi was religious—and that, apparently, damned the Indian leader completely'. He adds: 'No less than three times in a couple of hours the great man told me that Jesus was an illiterate peasant. I could have told him that the Galilean was, according to such records as we have, neither illiterate nor a peasant; but I was chiefly perplexed by the irrelevance of this intellectual snobbery. Even an illiterate peasant might have many things to teach the world, but what had Jesus, illiteracy or peasantry, to do with Gandhi, who was more often abused as a "crafty lawyer"?' Reginald came to the reluctant conclusion that the 'great intellectual merely said his piece because, like a schoolboy, he thought it would shock—also that his mind appeared to be incapable of clear, objective reasoning outside the field of mathematics. The chief political observation he made at the time was that the American Navy was the greatest force for peace in the world. As I watched his many political somersaults in later years—each a pragmatic reaction to some new but transient phenomenon—I often remembered that preposterous discussion.'

The great man nevertheless wrote kindly to Gandhi's *Angad* after that meeting, saying he had 'enjoyed our apparently argumentative talk', and that he thought they had 'underlying agreement', which, says Reginald, 'in a curious sense was true, though with regards to ends rather than means or principles'. Russell hoped the young man would visit Beacon Hill again, and, 'a matter of prime importance to me', Reginald wrote, 'he was a subscriber to my bulletin, *Indian Events*, issued at that time'. He had expected 'somebody intellectually overwhelming but with no feelings,' but instead he found a man 'who talked a great deal of nonsense but sometimes acted with what seemed to me a sound instinctive judgment, when he had put his calculations on one side'.

* In *My Life and Crimes*, 1956.

It is interesting that A. S. Neill impressed Reginald similarly, 'for I was always torn', he wrote, 'between irritation at the superficiality of some of his assertions in his writings on the one hand, and on the other a deep admiration for something like instinct which so often made him, as a pioneer in free education, do the right thing in a difficult situation'.

But Reginald, who had the just cause of the displaced and dispossessed Palestinian Arabs deeply at heart, as I have, would have saluted Bertrand Russell at the end for the last thing he wrote, on January 31, 1970, forty-eight hours before he died, which was a message to the International Conference of Parliamentarians held in Cairo in February, and in which he forthrightly pointed out that 'For twenty years Israel has expanded by force of arms. After every stage in this expansion Israel has appealed to "reason" and has suggested "negotiations". This is the traditional rôle of the imperial power, because it wishes to consolidate with the least difficulty what it has already taken by violence. . . . The tragedy of the people of Palestine is that their country was "given" by a foreign Power to another people for the creation of a new State. The result was that many hundreds of thousands of innocent people were made permanently homeless. With every new conflict their numbers have increased. How much longer is the world willing to endure this spectacle of wanton cruelty?'

At the end of the road he saw clearly and called for a 'new world campaign' to bring justice to the 'long-suffering people of the Middle East'.

It is of more importance to record this than offer a résumé of the wide-ranging but superficial conversation of that afternoon in the tower whose location I have long forgotten, in another life, in other worlds, long ago.

There was Freud, and A. S. Neill, and Bertrand Russell, and Dr. Marie Stopes, and Dr. Norman Haire—ringing the bells of freedom for the young intelligentsia of the amoral decade. Norman Haire was an eminent Harley Street gynaecologist, who made a great part of his considerable income from fitting the Gräfenberg inter-uterine ring, which was to the Twenties what the Pill is to the Seventies. Dr. Ernst Gräfenberg was a German Jew who had a thriving practice as a gynaecologist in Berlin, until the rise of the Nazis, when he left for America. He was a handsome man in his forties, of considerable personal charm, and in the late Twenties and early Thirties his surgery on the Kurfürstendamm was as busy as a railway station with women of all nationalities who came to be fitted with the new and infallible contraceptive device. Norman Haire was an Australian Jew, and a homosexual, and it is bitterly ironic that he had a tremendous feeling for Germany, which in those pre-Nazi days had a night life which catered diversely for homosexual tastes. Haire often declared that Germany was his spiritual home, and that when he retired he would settle there. Instead he fled back to Australia, where he was to die in 1952, when it was expected that Germany would invade England during World War II. Those who saw him off reported him as shaking like a leaf and hysterically declaring that he had 'so much to lose', which as a Jew he had, but so had some others of us who though we were not Jews were on the Nazi black list.

Haire wrote to me early in 1929 after the publication of my novel, *Crescendo*, that bad novel which one critic had called a 'saga of sex'. Haire was secretary of something called the World League for Sexual Reform, and he wrote to say that the novel had 'deeply moved and interested' him, and to ask if I would read a paper at the next conference of the League. I agreed to do this, and in the course of the correspondence he invited me to dinner at his Chinese house in Harley Street and to take the chair for him afterwards at a meeting of the Rationalist Press Association at which he was speaking on some aspect of sex. This I did, and from what I wrote about him in the *Confessions*, in a chapter which I subtitled 'Portrait of a Rationalist', it was a daringly outspoken occasion, leaving us all a little breathless, for at that time it was considered very uninhibited to say out loud in public such words as masturbation, homosexuality, orgasm.

At the time I greatly admired Norman Haire; in retrospect he seems a monster. He was very big, tall and broad, and with

E

a big belly from the gluttonous eating which was one of his chief pleasures. I wrote of him that seeing him eat was to be 'irresistibly reminded of the fairy stories of giants who could devour an ox as easily as other men devoured a cutlet'. He was a rabid teetotaller, and it was a point of pride with him that when he entertained, though he served very good food, very lavishly, he never at any time provided his guests with what he regarded as the rank poison of alcohol. He resented people commenting on his excessive eating, whereas, he said, if he drank excessively nobody would say anything; he insisted that all drinking was excessive, because even the smallest amount of alcohol in the bloodstream was bad.

I found his total rationality inhuman, and the grossness of his appetite where food and sex were concerned repugnant, but also I found him immensely amusing—which at that time was an overriding consideration. He could be kind, too; kind to me personally, and to the many people, rich and poor, whose sexual problems he sorted out free of charge. Certainly it was to his credit that in addition to his prosperous Harley Street practice he ran a birth-control clinic in the East End to which working-class women could come with their problems and receive help free or for very little.

We went a good deal to the theatre together—so much so that a woman cousin of his concluded we were having an affair. When I exclaimed at the preposterousness of the idea she assured me that I need not pretend with *her*—she was *delighted*, she said. When with some indignation I reported this to Haire he laughed and said he knew she believed this about us, 'and I encourage the idea!' I was shocked that he should use our friendship as a cover-up for his homosexuality, but even more—such was my youthful vanity—I resented that anyone should believe I would have an affair with such a Caliban.

His rationality could be monstrous. At the inquest on a mutual friend who had committed suicide he turned up wearing a silk scarf which had belonged to the dead man and smilingly asked me if I recognised it, which of course, distressed, I did. He was impatient of my distress; I was being sentimen-

tal, he said; it was a very good scarf; what was he supposed
to do with it—put it in the dustbin? Once in a discussion of
sex—his favourite subject—he asked me had I ever tried bes-
tiality, and in response to my reaction of horror asked calmly,
'Why not?' and added, with an amused smile, 'They say you
can train a peke to do anything!'

When I wrote my entirely adulatory piece about him I knew
all this, but did not mention it; he was amusing, he was kind,
he was progressive—that sacred word. 'He is a hedonist with
the courage of his convictions,' I wrote, warmly, 'and being
a gourmand is part of his hedonism, just as his hedonism is part
of his rationality.'

I thought the Chinese furnishings and decoration of his
Harley Street house very beautiful—certainly he possessed
many beautiful things—and considered Hugh Walpole stuffy
for being rude about them. In Haire's consulting room there
was a silver ceiling and the walls were hung with Chinese em-
broideries of birds and flowers on silk. In the dining-room all
was lacquer and dragons; in the drawing-room were Chinese
rugs, silken tapestries, gilded idols, and a blossoming almond
tree was painted on the ceiling. Later there was a similarly
furnished house in the country.

It was Haire who introduced me to W. B. Yeats, upon whom
he had just performed the Steinach rejuvenation operation.
The occasion was an invitation to dinner at the Harley Street
house; I was to put on my most alluring evening dress and all
my sex-appeal, for the famous poet to test out his rejuvenated
reaction to an attractive young woman, he said, blandly. I was
flattered, I suppose; certainly I counted it an honour to meet
Yeats, and I went along. It was an unconvivial, somewhat
strained occasion, for Haire was not interested in poetry, and
Yeats liked to drink very much more than he liked to eat, and
we left early and spent the rest of the night drinking burgundy,
after which Yeats was always at his raciest and most eloquent.
I have told something of the story of my friendship with W. B.
Yeats in *Privileged Spectator*, and it does not belong here in
this record of the Twenties. I met Haire in 1929, but I did not
meet Yeats until 1934. The friendship lasted until his death in

January, 1939. His last letter to me was written from the Hôtel
Idéal Séjour, at Cap Martin, where he died; it is dated December 23, 1938.* After his death I presented fifty of his letters to the Yeats Museum in Sligo.

In the Thirties I met Haire only occasionally, and less and
less. Our ideas and attitudes were poles apart and we ceased
to amuse each other; all that belonged to the Twenties.

In 1934 he edited an *Encyclopedia of Sexual Knowledge*,
about which a Negro friend, seeing a copy of it in my study,
exclaimed in awe, 'Are there really people who need an *encyclopedia* about it?'

---

* It is one of the several letters to me in Allan Wade's *The Letters of
W. B. Yeats*, 1954.

8

The clothes we wore

As though a league for reforming sex were not enough we had at the same time a Men's Dress Reform Society, with the same leading lights—Norman Haire, Miles Malleson, Professor J. C. Flugel.* There is in my album of snapshots taken in Oak Cottage garden at the end of the Twenties and the beginning of the Thirties a preposterous picture of Haire wearing knickerbockers, open-necked shirt, sandals. The society was very keen on open-necked shirts and sandals, because the essence of the reform was that dress had to be rational, and crowding the feet into shoes and encasing the neck in collar and tie was not. Shirts had also to be brightly coloured, because another part of the dress-reform programme was to get away from the conventional. For the evenings the dress-reform man wore a soft shirt, perhaps pleated, and a floppy bow tie, and he would not, of course, wear anything so orthodox as a dinner-jacket or tails, but a velvet jacket, preferably coloured. There was something to be said for the dress-reformers, though the movement was popularly associated with vegetarianism and crankiness, and long, Boy Scout shorts, wide, and down to the knee, did not help to convert the man-in-the-street.

No one was rash enough to attempt to include women in the dress-reform movement, and we wore our skirts daringly above

* Professor Flugel and his wife translated René Guyon's *Sex Life and Sex Ethics*, 1933, with an Introduction and Notes by Norman Haire.

the knee and dropped the hemline to the ankles as fashion dictated, with complete disregard for rationality.

Quite the most irrational item of women's dress in the mid-Twenties was the boudoir cap, which was a kind of mob cap of ruched lace and ribbon designed to be worn in the mornings for early tea. In hotels you did not admit the waiter or chambermaid to your room until you had pulled on a pretty boudoir cap. In your own home you put it on even if it was only your husband bringing the tea, or your twenty-five-bob-a-week 'cook general', always referred to as 'the maid'. Even if you had no husband and no maid you still put on a boudoir cap in the morning, 'first thing'. The 'drapery stores' displayed them in their windows, but with a few yards of narrow lace and ribbon and a bit of net you could make them yourself; there was a rosebud trimming you could buy by the yard and which was considered very fetching on a boudoir cap. Some of the boudoir caps sold in the shops were elaborate and expensive—they could cost as much as thirty-nine-and-six at a smart shop, and were described in the advertisements as wear 'for the smart bedroom woman'. I don't remember when they went out, but certainly the absurdity didn't follow us into the Thirties. In the Twenties, however, they were as essential to the feminine wardrobe as cami-knickers, of which we also aspired to possess a good many.

The cami-knicker was evolved from the camisole, which was a deep bodice which preceded the brassière. The camisole was not designed to lift the bosom but, on the contrary, to flatten it. Like boudoir caps they were fussily pretty, with a good deal of lace, and threaded with very narrow ribbon, in pink or blue, called 'baby ribbon'. When cami-knickers were invented the camisole disappeared, but we continued to be flat-chested and remained so until the invention of the 'bra' in 1929, when female curves became fashionable again. Cami-knickers were made of what we called 'Jap silk', though this was superseded by crêpe de Chine, a fabric greatly cherished. The most popular shade for *lingerie*, as we genteelly called underclothes, was pink. It might be vulgar—I seem to remember that the term was 'prostitute pink'—but we liked it. Pink crêpe de Chine cami-knickers . . . well, there are some very charming shades of pink, and crêpe de Chine was a soft and lovely material, and cami-knickers, combining two garments in one, were a sensible innovation; they were loose and comfortable, and they were pretty. On the stage it was the height of daring for an actress to appear in cami-knickers, but Ursula Jeans did so in a scene with the great matinée idol, Owen Nares, in *The Fanatics*, an outspoken play by Miles Malleson, in 1927, and Tallulah Bankhead did so in *The Garden of Eden*, by Avery Hopwood, also in 1927—a 'sensational' scene in which she ripped off her wedding-dress, a scene described as 'the wedding that does not come off, the dress that does'. In the first British talking film, *Blackmail*, directed by Hitchcock, in 1929, Anny Ondra, as the murderess, appeared in cami-knickers, knife in hand. So pretty and innocent the creatures looked in their cami-knickers, covering them down to the knee, it is difficult to understand now how this could ever have seemed so exciting.

Garters, too, were titillating. They were delicious concoctions of ribbon and rosebuds and lace, sometimes with a dashing touch of feather or marabout, excitingly glimpsed when the knees were crossed, and worn for no other purpose, it would seem, since our lovely shiny silk stockings were supported by suspenders. Though at the end of the decade, to be sure, with our hemlines round our ankles, knee-crossing did no one any good.

The fashions were ugly and stupid, as fashions in all ages invariably are, with our waistlines round the hips, making us appear shapeless creatures with neither busts nor waists, but when curves came back in 1929 clothes, paradoxically, became masculine, and the most heterosexual of women appeared in severely tailored suits worn with shirts and ties.

The cloche hat has become almost a symbol of the Twenties; it came down to our brows, almost enveloping us, but it was not unbecoming, I think, and we liked it; it stayed with us a long time; we wore it with our sacks of dresses and with our mannish suits; we wore it in town and in the country, and at tea-dances, and in our own homes at luncheon parties. Put-

ting on a hat to go down to one's own dining-room to lunch
with a few friends was idiotic, but it was the done thing so we
did it; just as the ladies withdrew at dinner parties at the end
of the meal, to go and powder their noses, as it was delicately
put, to be rejoined later by the gentlemen for coffee; just as
we fastened large and expensive sprays of artificial flowers to
the shoulders of our evening dresses—for so long as it was
the fashion. We were sexually emancipated, and we had the
vote, but we were not liberated from the tyranny of fashion
and social conventions. Our morals might be nowhere, but
when it came to fashion and etiquette we conformed. There
were various small niceties, too—we always offered both Turkish and Virginian cigarettes when we entertained, we served
finger-bowls with warm water and a slice of lemon, our coffee
sugar was coloured crystals, and we put out coloured matches
for those who wished to smoke—and the ladies, of course, all
smoked, conscientiously, as the outward and visible sign of
sex equality. Long cigarette holders became fashionable, and
in the early Twenties for those who had time to wear them
there were trousered 'smoking suits' for women. But I had
been initiated into the vice of smoking before the Twenties,
when I was working in the Charles F. Higham advertising
agency; a girl in the office with whom I became friendly
smoked, and she took me one evening after work to an underground tea place called The Cave where tea-for-two was served
in alcoves, and the lighting was dim, and *women smoked*.
The year would have been 1916 or 1917, not later. The girl,
whose name I remember as Monica, gave me a De Reszke
Turkish cigarette from a small packet, and there we two young
girls viciously sat, with our pot of tea and our toasted scones,
smoking, and *in public* . . . But it was, as I remember it, quite
some way into the Twenties before women smoked much in
restaurants. By the end of the decade, however, cigarette advertising was aimed at women—keep slim by smoking, instead
of eating between meals light a cigarette instead! That such
iniquitous advertising was permitted seems hard to credit now,
but the idea that lung cancer could be induced by smoking had
to wait for another forty years to emerge.

It interests me, in going through albums of snapshots taken here, there and everywhere, in the Twenties, to find myself never without a hat, whether it is sitting among the bracken in Richmond Park, standing beside a canal in Amsterdam, in the Forum at Rome, in front of a palm tree in Algiers, or anywhere else, and there are studio portraits galore, always with hat, cloche or 'picture', felt or straw, and one dashing piece of millinery that seems to be one huge bow of ribbon. A 'picture hat' press photograph, I note with awe, was marked—though not by me—'to be sent to forty newspapers'. . . .

9

Modernity in the home

It is horribly significant that when I moved into Oak Cottage in 1929 one of the first things I did was to throw out the handsome oxydised silver candelabra I had been bequeathed by the former owner and replace it by an inverted alabaster bowl, yellow and hideous, but very 'modern'. Like the chromium plate and black table, of cubistic design, which supported a cubistic lamp with a cubistic shade of spun glass. Very Jazz Age.

At the house of the willow tree I had let myself go more spectacularly, turning the room designed as the drawing-room into a blue-and-orange 'dance room', with a bar. That it was blue-and-orange instead of orange-and-black, the really modish colour scheme, showed at least a measure of non-conformity. There were Egyptian runners on the walls, orange-painted rush chairs and matching table, a black-and-orange rug—rolled up for dancing—long orange silk curtains at the windows, a blue-and-orange painted cabinet gramophone, which we wound up untiringly to play *Felix kept on walking, Thanks for the buggy-ride,* and *Yes, sir, that's my baby,* and other inspiriting numbers. That we could keep on winding up the gramophone for hours on end is the measure of our dance mania. We began the evening with cocktails—shaken with ice chipped from the block in the ice-box—and continued it with gin-and-ginger-beer, and freely flowed the gin at twelve-

and-six a bottle. We sang as we energetically charged about
the room :

> '*I want to* be *happy,*
> *But I won't* be *happy*
> *Till I've made* you *happy too-oo!*'

Friends came to dinner, there was coffee in the 'dance room',
then the orange-and-black rug would be rolled up, and the
gramophone wound up, and the real business of the evening
would begin.

At Oak Cottage we danced on the red-tiled floor of the
dining-room, pushing back the fumed-oak refectory table; there
were orange plates and an orange bowl, and orange curtains
at the windows. In the sitting-room the cabinet gramophone
had been lacquered black. Above the mantelpiece was a Van
Gogh print. The Sunflowers were very popular; they went
with the orange-and-black.

When the lamp shades were not yellow alabaster they were
of silk, with dangling tassels and fringes, but these were mostly
confined to bedrooms, for modernity was cube-shaped and
jazz-patterned; furniture and clocks and fireplaces were all
cubistic, angular, and carpets and cushions and lampshades
patterned with zigzag, jazz designs. Curves were out and an-
gles in. There were orange cushion-covers with black cats
appliqued to them; there were orange and yellow artificial
chrysanthemums and bright blue lupins, ideal for standing in
a tall papier-mâché vase in a corner of the dance room. There
was a lamp in the shape of a parrot, and a basketful of shell
flowers concealing an electric light bulb, both very effective
when lit up. I yearned for such things; I had seen them at my
boss's house in the country and in the big London stores, and
when money ceased to stand between me and their acquisition I acquired them. Whatever was modern was necessarily
good, and the influence of cubism on the furnishing and decoration of the home was considerable. Strangely, though, in
the novel that was inspired by the house of the willow tree,
Green Willow, the house was furnished with old furniture—

there was a 'mahogany bow-fronted chest-of-drawers with glass handles, inherited from her grandmother', a mulberry wood table, a big old bookcase, set off against bare painted walls and polished wooden floors. It would seem that despite all the intensive Jazz Age modernity with another part of myself there was nostalgia for the past, though resolutely suppressed at that time.

The 'hideous "modernism" of the late-Twenties home' was illustrated in a book entitled *Interiors*, by Margaret and Alexander Potter;* there is depicted an ugly square-tiled fireplace, a round table supporting a cocktail shaker, a standard lamp consisting of a steel tube surmounted by a square shade, a jazz-patterned rug, on the arm of a chair an ashtray fastened to a strip of leather, a completely hideous settee, a bowl suspended from the ceiling for a centre light, a two-coloured pouffe beside the settee, a dado round the ceiling, under the picture rail, and studying the whole ensemble you know that the colour scheme would have been orange-and-black. 'Modernism' interpreted by Suburbia was quite horrible; the dance room at the house of the willow tree was not like that, but rather raffish —or designed to be—though there was the jazz-patterned rug, to be sure, and the pouffe, brought back like the Egyptian runners from some cruise or other. Standard lamps, too, were all the rage, and a cocktail shaker, of course, as essential a piece of equipment for the home as a cabinet gramophone and a collection of dance records.

Domestic interior decoration was undoubtedly influenced by the posters on the London Underground, and elsewhere, designed by the modernistic artists of the times, such as McKnight Kauffer, Paul Nash, C. R. W. Nevinson, but what was striking and original in commercial art underwent something of a sea-change in the home.

All the same I should not have got rid of that chromium-plate-and-black-lacquer table; it would have been a period piece by now.

* 1957.

10

'Wild' parties

Strictly, the Bright Young Things were a small but much publicised social clique, some of them, as Richard Bennett points out in his book, *A Picture of the Twenties,** not so young, 'madcaps' whose idea of fun was to gate-crash parties, and who gained notoriety with a Babies' Ball, at which, in Bennett's words, 'the guests arrived in prams and got drunk in rompers, pinafores and sailor suits'. I doubt if anyone outside their own set found them amusing. But there was another sense in which all of us who were young in the Twenties, and enjoying what Douglas Goldring called our 'uninhibited fling' in the 'new morality', were bright young things, in the sense that we were young and we were gay and intent on enjoying the exciting new post-war world. We liked parties; we gave them and we went to them; we drank too much, I suppose, but we didn't go dressed as babies, or go in for pyjama parties, or treasure hunts by motor-car, or midnight bathing, and no one rode upstairs on a horse—we left all that to the Mayfair set. It cannot be said that we took our pleasures soberly, for that we did not, but I think it true to say we were a lot less 'wild' than some records of the Twenties might lead those who were not 'there' to suppose.

There were, as now, different kinds of parties. There were cocktail parties at which we just stood about and gabbled and babbled as people do at such parties today, but with this differ-

* 1961.

ence, that in the Twenties a cocktail party was a party at which you drank cocktails, whereas at the so-called cocktail parties of today, in my experience, the proffered drinks range from sherry to gin-and-tonic and whisky-and-soda, with never a cocktail in sight.

There were dance parties, which were really drinking parties, plus; and there were just parties, at which you met either for a sit-down meal followed by dancing, or for buffet snacks followed by dancing or not as you pleased, but which were, of course, drinking parties. The difference, I suppose, between the parties of the Twenties and those of today is that though you do just naturally drink you don't just naturally dance. There are twenty-first birthday parties at which, of course, the young people dance, and such parties don't really get going until the oldsters have either gone home or gone to bed. The young of course dance; the young will always dance—thank God!—but they certainly don't wind up any gramophones, or even plug them in, to do it; they go to discothèques and their own clubs, and of course to parties; but they are not permanently switched on as we who were young in the Twenties were. It was more laborious with us, but it was also probably more fun.

The parties at the house of the willow tree were decorous enough; nobody passed out or was sick, and in the morning some of us woke up with headaches, but in our own beds. At Oak Cottage we drank a good deal of gin, and talked, I suppose, a good deal of nonsense, being conscientiously amusing and outrageous, as the fashion was, and sometimes we danced. There was nothing 'wilder' than such a misconceived joke as releasing the brakes in the string of cars parked in front of the house so that they slid down the hill, bumping into each other; and sometimes people sneaked off from the party and got into the backs of cars—not always their own—for their own private petting party. Sheer high spirits, as you might say; all very silly, but not sillier than the goings-on of the Mayfair set, and at the time it all seemed fun—Terribly Amusing. It was, as I have said, relatively the Age of Innocence and we were easily amused.

To Oak Cottage in those days came Christina Foyle, Allen
Lane (how could we dream he would eventually become titled
and a millionaire?), Douglas Goldring, Violet Hunt, Louis
Marlow, and his novelist wife, Ann Reid—who was to die
young. Louis Marlow had just written a novel entitled *Love
by Accident*, and Ann Reid had written a novel called *Love
Lies Bleeding*. Later Marlow wrote a novel called *Swan's Milk*;
all pleasantly affected and literary. *Love by Accident* was described to me by Ralph Straus, the *Sunday Times* critic, who
was also a regular visitor to Oak Cottage, as being all about
a man who couldn't avoid women 'because every time he got
into bed he found one there'. It was the sort of witticism we
liked very much in the Twenties. Straus was an amiable and
pleasant man, with a passion for cricket; he was also the most
fantastic social snob. Once when I asked him what he was doing for Easter—or some such national holiday—he said he
was going to Argyll; I said it was a part of Scotland I didn't
know, to which replied, 'I mean the Duke . . .' God bless his
genial memory, for I was always sure of a good notice in the
Sunday Times as long as he lived. Violet Hunt was already
old and a little muddled by the time I met her. We were leaving
a party together once when she said to me, 'It was nice meeting
Ethel Mannin. She is such a little girl, isn't she?' I took the
line of least resistance and agreed with her. In 1932 she gave
me a copy of her book, *The Wife of Rossetti*, inscribing it, 'To
kind Ethel Mannin'.

Louis Marlow was brought to Oak Cottage by Douglas
Goldring, whose close friend he was; Ralph Straus I was taken
to meet by Comyns Beaumont, editor of the *Bystander*, and
uncle of Daphne du Maurier, who I was to meet later. Straus
had attacked *Crescendo*, the only bad review I ever had from
him, for he had far too strong a social sense to give his friends
other than good reviews. I wrote a good deal for the *Bystander*,
and when I mentioned to the editor Straus's derisory remarks
he said I had better meet him and take the war into the enemy
camp. He lunched us at Ciro's, very fashionable as a night
spot, but also fashionable by day, after which we never looked
back.

Daphne du Maurier also came to Oak Cottage, but that was in the early Thirties, and we are still here concerned with the Twenties, and those 'wild parties' which were in fact not wild at all, but gay—*toujours gai*. (Does anyone now remember Don Marquis' *archy and mehitabel,** I wonder—'*toujours gai archy and toujours the lady that is my motto*', says mehitabel the cat.)

But there were more serious parties. Literary parties given by the great American publisher, George Doran, at the Savoy Hotel, London. Then we were all dressed up and busy being geniuses together, as Bob McAlmon would say. George Doran subsequently amalgamated with Doubleday and became Doubleday Doran, but in the beginning he was just George Doran, who gave wonderful parties for his authors when he came to London. For the young author I then was it was a great honour to be on the same list as such famous and distinguished writers as Arnold Bennett, Somerset Maugham, Hugh Walpole, and to meet them in the flesh, and such brilliant young men of my own generation as Noël Coward and Beverley Nichols . . . who set down some impressions of his elders, in his much-discussed book, *Twenty-Five,*† as brashly and rashly as I was to do in my *Confessions*, though I think he didn't have to spend so many years living it down. By the time I met him he was no longer twenty-five and the book was behind him; my own major literary indiscretion was to come, and George Doran was one of the two people who counselled against it; the other was Michael Joseph, who was then at Curtis Brown's. George Doran was so convinced that the *Confessions* were a mistake that he published only a small edition of two thousand copies, 'sheets' from the English edition; it was not, that is to say, printed in America. Michael Joseph, who was my friend as well as my literary agent, declared that the book would 'ruin' me as an author, by which he meant irretrievably damage my literary reputation; its success, he warned, would be a *succès de scandale*, and I would never live

* 1931.
† 1926.

Ralph Straus,
most amiable of
literary critics,
at Oak Cottage
1934

Paul Tanqueray
and the author
at Oak Cottage,
1932

The author and her daughter, 1925

it down. My attitude, of course, was youthfully arrogant—'publish and be damned!'

But he and George Doran were right; I have never succeeded in living the book down. All over India in 1949 eager young Indians told me how much this book had meant to them, and as recently as 1970 a Pakistani earnestly assured me that the book had influenced a whole generation; he himself had read it as a young man some twenty years after publication. In 1969 it dogged me to the Isle of Dogs, on a tour of East End pubs, for a book I was writing,* when a man from New Zealand told me how 'thrilled' his wife would be that he had met me, because she 'thought the world of' one of my books . . . the *Confessions*. The book has been for many years out of print, but is of course still available at the libraries, and there are apparently people who still cherish it as one of the first Penguins . . . done at sixpence.

I first met Allen Lane at a literary dinner which he himself thought, when he wrote me shortly before his death in 1970, must have been a P.E.N. Club occasion. I was never a member of P.E.N. but the woman friend with whom I went to America in 1926 was, and members could take guests. Certainly it was she who introduced me to the incredibly good-looking young man I noticed at the other side of the room; I drew her attention to him, and she exclaimed, surprised that I did not know, 'But that's Allen Lane!' It seems strange to me, now, that I did not record in the *Confessions* how we met, but only wrote, frivolously, in the chapter on Ralph Straus, of how 'Mr. Allen Lane took me to the Authors' Club for dinner and told me to "dress quietly" and to remember that his mother would be there.' The injunction to dress quietly was probably provoked by a tendency to a flaunting scarlet, barebacked at that, when it came to evening dress. It is again the measure of our innocence at that time that it was as easy as that to be 'shocking'.

Allen Lane, and his brother, Richard, came to the parties at Oak Cottage, and we drank a good deal of gin, and we led each other on, and amused each other, and there was a certain amount of nonsense, but no one rode a horse up the stairs, and

* *England at Large*, 1970.

no one threw anyone in the lily pond, and around 1 a.m. there would be a great slamming of car doors and a starting up of engines, and if some of the young men who had driven out alone now had female passengers, it would surely have been unchivalrous to leave any young person to make her way home by public transport at that hour. We enjoyed ourselves, and as Mehitabel was always saying, what the hell. . . .

At one of the George Doran literary parties at the Savoy Hotel I sat next to Somerset Maugham. It would have been some time in 1927, for Doran had just published my fourth novel, *Pilgrims*, in America, where it had been described, embarrassingly, as 'another *Of Human Bondage*'. By no stretch of imagination could that immature novel of Paris and Amsterdam—and Bruges and Ghent—in the early Twenties be likened to Maugham's masterpiece, and I was probably over-anxious to dissociate myself from such nonsense, for re-reading now, in 1970, that account in my *Confessions* of that first conversation with Maugham it seems to me I talked as foolishly as that American reviewer, and that Maugham bore with it most patiently. For some reason I did not record what is much more interesting, and which is Maugham speaking to me on another Doran occasion about a new novel by a young friend of his, *Squirrel's Cage*.* Godfrey Winn's second novel, which he would like to help, he said, and if I could write about it anywhere, or tell people about it . . . Forty years on Godfrey Winn has been for decades probably the highest-paid journalist in the country, demonstrating an astonishing staying power. He wrote warmly and generously about 'Willie' Maugham after his death—which cannot be said of some who had as much reason to be grateful for Maugham's friendship and patronage in their youth.

I always admired Maugham very much as a story-teller, and still do, but though I met him several times in the late Twenties and early Thirties I cannot claim friendship; though he was once my guest at a dinner party I gave at Taglioni's, an Italian restaurant very fashionable at the time. There was no particular reason for giving that dinner party; it was not

* 1929.

given for Maugham especially; one just did give these restaurant parties occasionally. There was plenty of money around for the young and bright, and plenty of interesting people around, also, and any kind of party was fun.

I have long forgotten who else was at that party, but I remember Maugham, who sat at my right hand, as the guest of honour, speculating about the troupe of Russians who played and sang during the evening. 'If one knew their lives,' he said, broodingly; they would have been *émigrés*, White Russians. It impressed me as a demonstration of the mind of the born story-teller in action; people, whoever they were, would always arouse his imagination, were always potential material for a short story, whether he identified with them and was sympathetic to them or not, though in this case I felt that he was sympathetic. But if they had been Red Russians he would still have wondered about their backgrounds, I would think, for he was interested in people rather than in ideas, what they felt rather than what they thought or believed.

I ever had only three letters from him, I think, one of which was to thank me for that restaurant party, 'your wonderful party', and for asking him to it. It was written from London, in January, and concludes, 'Oh, the snowdrifts of Wimbledon Park and the frozen keys of the typewriter!'

Who remembers now the Chelsea Arts Ball on New Year's Eve at the Albert Hall? I don't mean the attempted revival of it in the Fifties, but its heyday in the Twenties and early Thirties, the great annual fancy-dress party? I never had any feeling for fancy dress, and never indulged in it even on shipboard on those cruises; it always seemed to me embarrassing and I could never overcome that self-consciousness. I even found the spectacle of friends in fancy dress somehow embarrassing—the feeling that they were making fools of themselves, behaving childishly. But I was roped in by a friend for the Chelsea Arts Ball on New Year's Eve, 1928, and having been assured that fancy dress was not obligatory went along. I have remembered it as hot, noisy and crowded, and altogether too boisterous. But two things I have remembered from

it : being taken to a box to meet Walter Hutchinson, my publisher, and being asked by him in the course of conversation
whether I was on his 'list'—he had the reputation for being
more interested in race-horses than authors, and it was a point
of pride with him that he had never read a book. He did not
meet his authors more than he could help, and this was the
first of the only two occasions I ever did meet him.

The other memory of the Chelsea Arts Ball was the anguished cry of an attractive young actress, when the last
note of the Old Year had chimed, 'O God, another year of
sleeping alone!'

II

The books we read

In retrospect it seems that when we were not reading Galsworthy—those everlasting Forsytes—in the Twenties we were, at the other pole, reading Aldous Huxley—all those ranting males going on about sex, society, art, religion, always the same character bobbing up under a different name, in *Crome Yellow, Antic Hay*, and at the end of the decade, *Point Counterpoint*. Did the same people read both Galsworthy and Huxley? I think so. I certainly did, and the people I knew seemed to. In 1922 the Forsyte novels, beginning with *The Man of Property*, first published in 1906, and ending with *To Let*, published in 1921, came out in one volume under the title of *The Forsyte Saga*. But it was not the end of the Forsytes; in 1924 appeared *The White Monkey*, the first of a trilogy, the other two being *The Silver Spoon*, 1926, and *Swan Song*, 1928. Soames Forsyte appears in all of them. Galsworthy himself, writing in 1922, in a preface to *The Forsyte Saga*, says that 'it cannot be absolved from the charge of embalming the upper middle-classes'. Yet so many of us, so very far removed from the upper middle-classes, waded through the salt waters of the Saga—Galsworthy's own description again—and felt pity and sadness, were moved, and, quite simply, loved it all. Just as forty years on a generation that had never read the novels loved it all on television. I read the novels at the time, all of them, but I do not think I could read them now, and I haven't television. The only authors I seem able to re-read are Conrad and Maugham—the one who was never easily readable, and the other so very readable.

But it was not *The Forsyte Saga* which was 'the best-seller of the year' in 1922, but A. S. M. Hutchinson's novel of much less grand people, *If Winter Comes*. It was a very moving novel, and, as I have said, with all our Jazz Age sophistication we were sentimental at heart. We were moved by *If Winter Comes* in 1922 as we were by Margaret Kennedy's *The Constant Nymph* in 1924, but it was Michael Arlen's *The Green Hat*, published in the same year, which was the year's literary sensation. The novel was considered 'cynical, ruthless and daring'; it became a best-seller; it was made into a film and into a play. Katharine Cornell played in it on Broadway, and Tallulah Bankhead in London. Greta Garbo and John Gilbert played in the film. It was romantic melodrama; preposterous nonsense. It was exciting, all the same; daring—V.D. came into it. James Agate wrote of the play : 'This piece has no significance of any kind. It takes the spectator into an over-nourished, over-dressed, over-laundered, over-sexed world and exhibits a heroine equally sensual and witless.'

I did not see the play, and down through the years I have always written off the novel as trivial; looking at it again now I do not think it trivial, and certainly not cynical. It is lush, over-written, melodramatic, basically absurd, because people don't talk like that, act like that, react like that; but I think now that in the creation of his heroine, Iris Storm, *demi-mondaine* as one character in the book calls her, a 'house of men' as she calls herself, Michael Arlen set out to establish a point which greater writers than he—de Maupassant comes to mind—have thought it worth establishing, which is that such a woman can have integrity, courage, unselfishness to the point of the quixotic. She is Mrs. Storm when the novel opens, but at the age of nineteen she had married a beautiful young man just down from Oxford, Boy Fenwick, 'the most gifted of God's creatures'. She had married him without being in love with him because the father of the man with whom she was in love, Napier Harpenden, would not countenance his son marrying into the de-

generate March family, Gerald March, Iris's beloved twin
brother, being an alcoholic, and Iris unchaste. Boy Fenwick
catches Iris on the rebound, but in the dawn after the wedding
night he throws himself from a window of the hotel at Deauville where they were to spend the honeymoon. Iris declares
that he died 'for purity' letting it be thought that he committed
suicide in horror at the revelations of her past. In this way
Gerald is allowed to keep his illusion as to the character of his
friend, Boy. She plunges into a life of sexual debauchery after
that, 'and when four years later young Storm married her,
against his people's wishes, she was no more than—well, what
do you call those people? *Demi-mondaines?* And since Storm's
death . . .' Hector Storm, like Boy Fenwick, had loved Iris ex-
travagantly—she wasn't 'one of those women you love a little'.
Iris seduces her great lover, Napier, three days before his wedding, and nearly dies in childbirth later as a result. In the great
showdown at the end, the powerful, passionate, reconciliation
scene between Iris and Napier's father and Napier's wife, it
is Napier who reveals that Boy Fenwick committed suicide because he knew when he married Iris he had syphilis and the
enormity of what he had done overcame him, and drove him
mad. Iris knew this, but gave out that he had died 'for purity'
so that Gerald might go on having his 'little tin-god hero'.
Napier speaks out at the end because he loves Iris and is
'damn well going to have these people respect you as I do. . . .'
(There are a lot of dots in this book.) In all the brouhaha that
follows this sensational revelation Napier would have gone off
with Iris, but she sends him back to his wife, Venice, by telling
him what she had promised her not to tell, which is that Venice
is going to have a child. 'Do you think I can leave you when
you are going to have a child of mine,' Napier says, when he
returns. Venice sobs that 'She's sent you back to show you she
loved you more than I do . . .' Whilst all this is going on there is
the roar of Iris's yellow Hispano-Suiza. 'The distant roar still
filled the room like a menace.' The men, including Napier's
father, rush off after the Hispano. But Iris drives deliberately
into a great tree she and her brother had loved as children,
choosing 'the only way to make it look like an accident'.

The sheerest melodrama, and absurd. As young Fenwick knew when he married Iris that he had syphilis why should he suddenly go mad with remorse and commit suicide? The damage had by then been done, though we are not told whether in fact Iris contracted the disease. And why should it be assumed when Iris drove off, after sending Napier back by telling him about Venice, that she intended to kill herself in the car? It's all false, nonsense, both the things said and the things done, and yet with all that absurdity and falsity it does contrive somehow to be moving—something that the author wanted to say about goodness somehow gets through. Or so I think, forty years and more on.

Michael Arlen was the pen-name of Dikran Kouyoumidjan, whose family fled from Armenia at the time of the first Turkish massacres; they went to Bulgaria, where Dikran was born. Three years later the family moved on to England, to settle in Lancashire and set up in small businesses, in the Armenian way. They were neither rich nor poor, but they were all right; they prospered; they could afford to send young Dikran to a good school, and he had a spell in Edinburgh University, where he was to study to be a doctor, but he left after three months to become a free-lance journalist in London. His son has written a book about his parents, *Exiles*.*

Dikran Kouyoumidjan's first book was a collection of sketches about London which he called *The London Venture*, and which Heinemann published. He changed his name at his publisher's suggestion, and invented Michael Arlen. The book was published in 1920, when he was twenty-four years old. He lived, then, in a small room over a shop in Shepherd Market, Mayfair, and worked very hard and had no money. *The Green Hat* he wrote in Lancashire, in his parents' little house in Manchester; he wrote it in two months. He had written and published several novels and collections of short stories before then. He married a Greek countess, Atalanta Mercati, when he was twenty-nine and an established success—Michael Arlen, the author of *The Green Hat*. He called his son Michael, and

* 1971

in *Exiles* this son, Michael J. Arlen, has written what *Time* magazine (June 8, 1970) calls a 'scrupulously personal book. ... uncharted miles away from Father's evanescent *Young Men in Love,* or *These Charming People*'.

The son's account of the Kouyoumidjan family in exile, his parents, his father's retirement from the literary scene in the Thirties when his vogue was over, and his death from cancer at the age of sixty in 1963, is deeply moving. In his introduction to a reprint of *The Green Hat* which Cassell's published in 1968, A. S. Frere, who knew Michael Arlen well, says that 'time and again', in New York in the post-war years, he tried to get him to agree to the reprinting of his books, but that stubbornly he refused. 'He thought nothing of his own work,' Frere writes, 'he had written for and about people and times that were better dead and gone.' He adds, 'Of course he was wrong. I thought so then and I think so now.' Nevertheless there was very little demand for the reprint of *The Green Hat,* and his son tells me that the proposed reprinting referred to paperbacks which had not then evolved into the respectable form of publishing they are today. 'He used to say *then*', his son writes me, 'that he didn't want to come out in paperback, although I think he'd change his mind today.' He adds, categorically, 'It was never a question of hard-cover publishers suggesting new editions, and of his turning them down. He would have been delighted. In fact, there was no apparent demand for his books, and no publisher I know ever suggested another edition. *That* knowledge—that there was so small a demand for his books—was one (but only one, I imagine) of the facts that turned him into a non-writer.'

For his part, Michael Arlen liked to say—as quoted by his son in *Exiles*—'I have the affection of my wife, the tolerance of my children and the friendship of head waiters. What more do I need?'

It was one of his little airy speeches, his son tells us, like the one about how he had always said that when he had X amount of money he would retire, 'And as things turned out, I eventually had X amount of money. And retired. And lived happily ever after.' The son adds, 'He seemed to be living happily ever after, too, although in truth I don't remember his having any friend close enough in those days to know the difference. Or any friend he would let that close to him.' He would hear his father pacing up and down in his study at nights in those New York days, and 'the walls must have seemed unbearably close at times'.

A literary friend of mine who met him in New York, at various Manhattan parties, tells me that because he himself, as a newspaper man, was very busy at that time he envied Michael Arlen's capacity 'for being perfectly happy doing absolutely nothing'. Perhaps for a time he was; perhaps he was resolved to be. For ten years he paced up and down at night in that room full of books, including his own, and in which writing material was laid out, and in which he never wrote. That brief success in the Twenties had given him what he wanted in material terms; it had been a brilliant decade for him and he had enjoyed it hugely; it had given him, too, the means to 'retire', when he had to, in the darkening Thirties, and did so with a most admirable dignity and a quite poignant courage.

In the Twenties Michael Arlen was as much a part of the scene, as a personality and as a writer, as the Bright Young Things, the Mayfair set, about whom he wrote so entertainingly. Paul Tanqueray, who was one of the fashionable portrait photographers of the era, told me : 'I used to see Arlen at first-nights—he in the stalls, I in the pit. I was only twenty when I saw Tallulah Bankhead in the play of *The Green Hat*, and thought it very daring.' I never saw him myself, but his pictures were around, for he was well publicised in the gossip columns, and he was undoubtedly a handsome man, in his Levantine fashion, with his well-shaped head, his thick wavy dark hair, brushed back from a high forehead, the small moustache, and he was always very well groomed. He looked, really, what the author of a best-selling sophisticated novel could be expected to look like. He was seen around in all the smart places and in the company of beautiful women. It was all part of being Michael Arlen, and he enjoyed being Michael Arlen, and why not? He had worked hard and got there by his own efforts—come up the hard way, as we should say nowadays, the dark, foreign-looking young man with the Manchester background of Armenian small business men. He was ambitious, and he had courage and stamina under that glossy exterior—more than we knew. He had the courage to fade out when his glittering world collapsed into the greyness of the Depression in the Thirties, and to do so with an air, 'all those airy little speeches' he used to make about his 'retirement', as his son tells us; and then his courage at the end, when death had him by the throat, and he knew it.

As a young writer I envied him; I had done nothing much myself by 1925, two novels only; he was four years my senior, and though I met so many people in the Twenties and early Thirties our paths did not cross. I doubt if we would have had, then, much to say to each other if they had. We inhabited different worlds, were quite differently orientated; I did not want his kind of green-hat success; I wanted, desperately, to be a 'serious' writer. In the Thirties Arlen did write some serious books, but, his son tells us, nobody liked them much. Who has heard, now, of the one into which he put a good deal of intelligent thought and imagination, *Man's Mortality*? Even his contemporaries have to rake around in their memory for something else he wrote beside *The Green Hat*, and then they come up with *These Charming People*, the short stories written earlier. *The Green Hat* was both the beginning and the end of his success, which now, in retrospect, seems a pity. But both he and his work were highly relevant to the period.

The Green Hat was sophisticated melodrama, and the language was often highflown to the point of absurdity—'There are dreams and there are beasts. The beasts walk glittering up and down the soiled loneliness of desire, the beasts prowl about the soiled loneliness of regret'—but Arlen was without the literary pretentiousness of Ronald Firbank, whom it was fashionable to admire, and who also was considered daring, with his 'little lilac sailor boys'. The novel we knew in 1929 as *Prancing Nigger* was first published in this country in 1925 as *Sorrow in Sunlight*. Firbank's nonsense was of a more literary order than Arlen's, and people too highbrow to read *The Green Hat* de-

lighted in it : 'Ever so lovely are the young men of Cuna-Cuna
. . . but none so delicate, charming and squeamish as Charlie
Mouth.' Charlie is the 'prancing nigger' of the story; parading
along the evening street, with a Pompadour fan borrowed from
his mother, 'little did that nigger boy know as he strolled along
what novel emotions that promenade held in store!' Seized
with a thirst for sherbet he comes to a square noted for the
frequency of its bars, their names, in flickering lights, showing
palely forth . . . and provoking a lyric ecstasy in the author:
'Cuna! City of Moonstones; how faerie art thou in the blue
blur of dusk!' He goes into a bar where, 'seated before a cloudy
cocktail, a girl with gold cheeks like the flesh of peaches', ad-
dresses him softly from behind, 'Listen, lion!' But he only smiles
at himself in the mirror. There are 'red roses against tall mir-
rors, reflecting the falling night'; and 'a fragrance of aromatic
cloves . . . a mystic murmur of ice'. Outside, the sky is all prim-
rose and silver pink.

It was literary affectation, of course, but the posturing was
deliberate. Life, for Firbank, was ironic comedy masking a hidden anguish, and all subtly veneered with Roman Catholicism
and a latent homosexuality. Ernest Jones, in an Introduction to
Three Novels by Ronald Firbank (*Vainglory, Inclinations,
Caprice*), brought out in 1950, declared of him that he was
a 'better and more serious writer than it has ever been fashionable to suppose' (which could have been said of the later
Michael Arlen), and he deplored the 'tiresome adulation of the
claque which adores his *fin-de-siècle* wickedness'. But it was
precisely that wickedness, that Wildean decadence, that so en-
chanted us in the Twenties—the subtly suggested viciousness of
the little lilac sailor boys, the intimated depravity of the 'love-
lilac' sleeves; the very titles fascinated us—*Prancing Nigger,
Valmouth, The Flower beneath the Foot*. I had them all—and
still have them, though I can no longer read them—and I loved
them. The flowery language, the decadence, the *fin-de-siècle*
naughtiness—it was delicious. An 'image of a little fisher-
boy in bathing drawers', the Hon. 'Eddy' Monteith in his bath,
'lying amid the dissolving crystals while his man-servant deftly
bathed him', Mademoiselle de Naziani and her bedtime prayer,

'Oh! help me heaven to be decorative and to do right! Let me always look young, never more than sixteen or seventeen— at the *very* outside . . .' Such joys there were in *The Flower beneath the Foot*, for those of us who reckoned to be culturally a cut above *The Green Hat* sophisticates.

But whilst the Firbank novels amused us, and a certain *chic* attached to an enjoyment of them, the early novels of Aldous Huxley, *Crome Yellow, Antic Hay, Point Counterpoint*, meant very much more to us. Douglas Goldring says that they 'amused, stimulated and charmed' us, and that they 'have since made, the Twenties glamorous for several generations of intelligent young people in London and the provinces', adding that 'no such blend of talent, wit, refined smut and erudition had been seen before, except in Norman Douglas's *South Wind*, to which novel, as some observed, the touch of genius, the one thing missing in Huxley's books, was added.' He found that touch, that 'indefinable something', discernible in the best of Firbank. I have an unbounded admiration for *South Wind*, but it was never a part of the Twenties scene; it was first published in 1910 and not reissued until 1935, and I did not myself read it until much later, though I had had the honour and pleasure of meeting Norman Douglas in Paris in the early Thirties. Firbank belonged in spirit more to the 1890's than to the Twenties, whereas Huxley was quintessentially of the Twenties. For *Crome Yellow* in 1921 I was not quite ready, but *Antic Hay* in 1923 was a tremendous intellectual excitement; there had been, as Douglas Goldring said, nothing quite like it before; there had been George Bernard Shaw, of course, saying devastating things for as long as one could remember, about marriage, religion, politics, but this was something different, a sardonic interpretation of the contemporary scene. *Antic Hay* is really a quite horrible book, about entirely dislikable people, vicious because they are bored; it is easy to understand how sensational it would all have been in the Twenties; what is not easy to understand is why so many of us found it so amusing. Rosie and her pink underclothes, Gumbril and his Patent Small-Clothes, the frightful Mr. Boldero with whom he goes into partnership— 'there are few who would not rather be taken in adultery than in provincialism'—the pneumatic trousers—'English trousers filled with English air, for English men'—which would sell because they were new—'the most absurd and futile objects can be sold because they're new'. This kind of sardonic humour was new, and in the Twenties whatever was new was acceptable— more than that, was admirable. We were not shocked by the sex scenes in *Antic Hay*; we were too resolutely modern to allow ourselves to be; we left that to people like James Douglas; we were the new generation and these were the new ideas—even though with another part of ourselves we responded emotionally to *My Heart Stood Still*.

It was with this part of ourselves that we responded to the novel, *Precious Bane*, by Mary Webb, the 'Shropshire authoress', once it had been boosted at a literary dinner by the Prime Minister, Mr. Stanley Baldwin. No one had taken much notice until then, but after the Prime Minister's acclaim—a copy had been sent to him at Downing Street—it became the best-seller of 1924, far and away eclipsing E. M. Forster's *A Passage to India*, and John Galsworthy's *The White Monkey*, also published that year; it sold nearly three-quarters of a million copies.

I was among those who bought it, read it, and loved it. The note is set by the author's foreword: 'To conjure, even for a moment, the wistfulness which is the past is like trying to gather into one's arms the hyacinthine colour of the distance. But if it is achieved, what sweetness!—like the gentle, fugitive fragrance of spring flowers, dried with bergamot and bay.' The key is maintained, from the opening sentence, 'It was at a love-spinning that I saw Kester first', to the final sentence, '. . . he [Kester] bent his comely head and kissed me full on the mouth'. The book is intensely poetic, in the Richard Jefferies (*The Story of my Heart*) fashion, full of the sights and sounds of Nature at her sweetest; water-lilies on a pool are 'like white and gold birds, sleeping, head under wing, or like summat carven out of stone', and it is as though Jesus, walking on the water, had laid them there 'with His cool hands'. The story is told in the first person by the heroine, a farm woman called Prudence Sarn, and in dialect. Her brother's name is Gideon, and he is in love with

Jancis, 'that was so beautiful', and with whose 'love-spinning' the story opens. It was from this that Stella Gibbons got the idea for her skit on the earth-earthy novel, *Cold Comfort Farm*, published in 1932. In this novel, it may be remembered, the author obligingly put asterisks to indicate her purple passages : 'The country for miles, under the blanket of the dark which brought no peace, was in its annual tortured ferment of spring growth; worm jarred with worm and seed with seed. Frond leapt on frond and hare on hare.' Etc. It was great fun. The men were all strong and coarse, interested only in the bed and board; they had powerful names, too—Adam and Seth and Reuben; and the family name, of course, was Starkadder. No one could write a *Precious Bane* after that.

We had, of course, the mocking brilliance of Evelyn Waugh's *Vile Bodies*, and *Decline and Fall*, about which we all raved, and which we did, I think, genuinely enjoy. They, too, like the Huxley novels, were something new. I had them and at the time was amused by them, but during one of my periodic book clearances threw them out and am now left with only his *A Handful of Dust*, published in 1934, which I still think very highly of. Douglas Goldring said that Evelyn Waugh was a disciple of Firbank, and possessed of that same 'indefinable something' which is genius, and which Huxley lacked, but with this I do not agree; Goldring wrote in 1945, by which time Huxley had produced a body of work of a brilliance and profundity which left Firbank and Waugh nowhere. The early Huxley was not profound, but he was brilliant, and his novels expressed what Ronald Blythe in his book on the Twenties and Thirties, *The Age of Illusion*,* calls the 'higher irreverence in literature'. As he says, 'the novels of Evelyn Waugh and Aldous Huxley weren't nice but they were fabulously funny and anti-cant'.

The two great literary excitements of the Twenties, I suppose, were the banning of *The Well of Loneliness* in 1928, and the publication in the same year of D. H. Lawrence's *Lady Chatterley's Lover* by Orioli in Florence, forbidden copies of which

* 1963.

filtered through to London, along with the later American pirated copies. I had a copy of this Orioli edition and attached so little value to it that it sat on the open bookshelves, with the rest of Lawrence's novels, and was read by so many people who came to the house, that by the time I came to sell it to America, when it was finally done here as a Penguin and became 'all the rage', its spine was broken, poor thing, and I got less for it than I otherwise would have. I have never regretted selling it; I needed the money, and though I defended the book passionately in 1928 in later years I came to think it was not really a very good novel, certainly nothing like as good as *Sons and Lovers*, and *The Plumed Serpent*, but novelettish, and the sexual antics rather silly, and all the ranting about sex and the good life intolerable. But I sincerely admired it at the time and it was important to defend it, and strongly, for Lawrence had set out to 'purify' sex, to demolish it as what he called a 'dirty little story', and he was passionately sincere. The police seizure of his poems, *Pansies*, was puerile, for they did not even contain the forbidden fornicatory words. Equally puerile was the seizure of some of the paintings, and copies of the book in which they were reproduced. But even at the end of the decade the puritans were still active amongst us. Whether Lawrence was possessed of genius or not he was intensely important to my generation, for, as I wrote of him in *Confessions*, his preoccupation with sex was a preoccupation with life; he wanted that we should be educated to life, instead of to earn and to spend. He ranted and he talked a good deal of nonsense, but also he said things that needed to be said at that time, and he said them explicitly and fearlessly. We who were young then were as indignant that *Lady Chatterley* was forbidden here as we were over the persistent puritanical attacks on Epstein's sculptures. I said my own angry piece about it in the *Confessions* : 'We have Jacob Epstein and D. H. Lawrence and we persecute them both. Truly there is no health in us.' I was wrong about that, though, for if there had been no health in us there would have been no protest, and protest there was.

Michael Arlen's son says in *Exiles* that his father used to go and see Lawrence in the country when he was very young and

Thamar Karsavina as she appeared in a Russian dance during
her American tour, 1924

Daphne du Maurier, 1932 *(Compton Collier)*

Reginald Reynolds at Oak Cottage, 1937. We married the following year

beginning as a writer, taking along stories he was writing, and deferring to him greatly, and Lawrence would advise him, and that in later years Arlen remembered this with satisfaction and pride. I did not know until I read it in *Exiles* that Lawrence put Arlen into *Lady Chatterley* as 'Michaelis', the Irish writer who was her ladyship's lover before the game-keeper, Mellors. I find myself wondering how many people knew this, and what Arlen himself thought of it, for as a fiction character 'Michaelis' is absurd. In the first place no Irishman was ever called Michaelis, and no Irishman was ever that foreign. It was as absurd for Lawrence to have 'disguised' the Armenian Michael Arlen as an Irishman as for me to have presented Bob McAlmon, essentially American, as a 'wild Australian' in *All Experience*. There are disguises that just don't fit. Michaelis is a young Irishman who had made a large fortune by his plays in America and been taken up 'quite enthusiastically for a time by smart society in London, for he wrote smart society plays'. He has an apartment in Mayfair, and 'walked down Bond Street the image of a gentleman', but when he goes to stay with the quality, in the person of Sir Clifford and Lady Chatterley, although he looks 'absolutely Bond Street' Sir Clifford's county soul recoils, for 'he wasn't exactly . . . not exactly . . . in fact he wasn't at all, well, what his appearance intended to imply'. Also Michaelis wasn't an Englishman, obviously; he had the wrong sort of face and bearing. This, of course, is ridiculous, and makes one wonder if Lawrence ever met an Irishman. Michael Arlen did look foreign; an Armenian does not look like an Englishman; but is an Irishman so different in appearance from an Englishman? Lawrence gives this travesty of an Irishman a Greek manservant and an inclination to marry a 'Turk or something . . . something nearer to the Oriental', since he feels he can't marry an Englishwoman or an Irishwoman. Though eventually he wants to marry Connie, Lady Chatterley. He is not much of a lover, and is altogether a somewhat inferior person, an outsider; but the sexual insensitivity—brutality, even—which Lawrence finally attributes to him is completely out of character and absurd; exit Michaelis—Lawrence had to get him off-stage for the entry of the Noble Savage in the person of the game-

G

keeper, who, of course, is entirely adequate. In my opinion all the characters in this novel are off-true and just not believable.

This seems to me, now, also the case with Richard Aldington's *Death of a Hero*, published in 1929, which was another great tirade about sex and cant—except when it gets to the war scenes, and then it is real; the ranting continues, but to more purpose, and the hero at one point, lying under canvas in a rest camp, reflects bitterly on the tragedy and futility of war: ' "The war to end wars !" Is anyone so asinine as to believe that ? A war to breed wars, rather . . .' And how right that reflection was !

In a dedicatory letter to his friend, Halcott Glover, Aldington called the novel a threnody, 'a memorial in its ineffective way to a generation which hoped much, strove honestly, and suffered deeply'. The book has passages and sentences represented by asterisks—a form of censorship to which Aldington submitted rather than delete what was at the time considered objectionable. It seemed to him 'better for the book to appear mutilated than for me to say what I don't believe'.

The other great post-war novel of the Twenties, R. H. Mottram's *The Spanish Farm,* published in 1924, probably stands up better to the test of time (Henry Williamson's *The Patriot's Progress*, and *The Good Soldier Schweik*, by the Czech writer, Jaroslav Hasek, both of which were much admired, came later, in 1930). I think the reason for this is that it doesn't rant; the case against war which it embodies is allowed to speak for itself. John Galsworthy said in his preface to it that it exhibited a new form, 'distinct even in this experimental epoch'. It was not precisely a novel, he wrote, not yet altogether a chronicle, and 'one might perhaps best call it highly humanised history'. It is that, but to those of us who read it and immensely admired it and were deeply moved by it in the Twenties it was, simply, a great novel of human beings caught up in the only recently over war. The French girl, Madeleine, of the Spanish farm in Flanders, dominates the book, and it is the story of her war-time love-affair with an English soldier; at the end of the war when, inevitably, he leaves her to return to England and she is alone she realises that she had never really wanted him, nor any Englishman, nor anything English. 'He was just one of the things the War, the cursed War, had brought on her . . .' The book concludes with the sorrowful and warning words, 'And as there was a Madeleine, more or less, widowed and childless, bereaved and soured, in every farm in north-eastern France, she became a portent. . . . For she was perhaps the most concrete expression of humanity's instinctive survival in spite of its own perversity and ignorance. There must she stand, slow-burning revenge incarnate, until a better, gentler time.'

Arnold Zweig's war novel *The Case of Sergeant Grischa** also won great acclaim. Indeed, J. B. Priestley declared it 'the greatest novel on a war theme that we have had from any country'.

Robert Graves' book, *Goodbye to all That*, was published in 1929 and was a tremendous success. He calls it 'an autobiography'; it is primarily a war book, but it covers his childhood and youth, and his years at Charterhouse, where his career as poet began, and where in his last year he edited *The Carthusian* with Nevill Barbour. He and Nevill Barbour both opposed the motion in the school debate, that 'this House is in favour of compulsory military service'. He says in his book that 'Nevill Barbour and I are, I believe, the only ones who survived the war', and at least one in three of his generation at school were killed. In 1914 he was nineteen and, he says, he forgot his pacifism and enlisted, 'ready to believe the worst of the Germans'. By the end of the war he was filled with misgivings as to the future, whether a lasting peace would be established as the result of the fearful sacrifice of young lives, and whether the arbitrament of war did not cause more evil than it destroyed, for both victor and vanquished. He tells us in *Goodbye to All That* that among those young writers who like himself had had firsthand experience of the war and emerged from it to voice similar misgivings were 'Osbert and Sacheverell Sitwell, Herbert Read, Siegfried Sassoon, Wilfred Owen', and, he adds, 'most other young writers of the time, none of whom now believed in the war'. Pacifism was very strong in 1928—though by the early Thirties it was already necessary to refer to 'ex-pacifists'—which

* 1927.

was when Graves was writing his book. It is interesting that both Aldington and Graves left the writing of their war books until some ten years after the war was over, and Henry William-son left his, *The Patriot's Progress,* even longer.

I bought Graves' book at the time, and it spoke very strongly to my own strong pacifism, and certainly as a picture and an indictment of the 1914–18 War it is of very great value; but looking at it again in 1970 I find myself raising an eyebrow over Graves' attitude to 'the natives' in Egypt when, on T. E. Law-rence's advice, he accepted a post as professor of English litera-ture in the newly founded university in Cairo in the mid-twen-ties. The young Professor Graves had two Sudanese servants to look after him and his wife and children, and though they had been 'warned' about 'native servants' they found these two 'temperate, punctual, respectful', and to his knowledge they never stole anything except the remains of a single joint of mut-ton. It is a defence of the 'native', of course, but also it has that condescension which characterised the white man's attitude to 'the natives' in the days of Empire. Mr. Graves never learned to speak Arabic, and found that all the best things in Egypt were dead. He soon packed the job up, and on the way back to Eng-land Venice after Cairo 'seemed like Heaven'. Perhaps his friend T. E. Lawrence had prejudiced him against Egypt, for he had written him before he sailed : 'The Egyptians . . . you need not dwell among them. Indeed, it will be a miracle if an Englishman can get to know them.' The country was beautiful, Lawrence wrote, the things admirable, 'the beings curious and disgusting'.

I cannot remember taking exception to any of this when I read the book at the time of its publication, but at that time I was more concerned with anti-militarism than with anti-imperialism. I had yet to meet Reginald Reynolds—already by then with Gandhi in India—and be awakened to the reality of the Indian struggle for independence, and Egypt was merely the place where the Pyramids and Sphinx were. I had a roman-tic admiration for T. E. Lawrence at that time—his *Revolt in the Desert,* a popular abridgement of his *Seven Pillars of Wis-dom,* issued in a limited edition in 1926, had been published in

1927. It was not to be for some years, and the advent of Reginald Reynolds into my life, that I was to meet the great Arabist, Nevill Barbour, and begin to understand and be interested in the problems of the Middle East, vis-à-vis the British and French mandates in their countries—which were all the Arabs got out of Lawrence's exploitation of their revolt against the Ottoman Empire to help secure Allied victory in that most dreadful, because so intensely personal, First World War, in which young men were trained to hate and in which almost a whole generation died.

Virginia Woolf's early novels came out in the Twenties, *Jacob's Room* in 1922 and *To the Lighthouse* in 1927, both of which I bought at the time, as befitted a serious young writer, and both of which I still possess, together with some of her later works. It would be nice to be able to report the proper intellectual excitement over this leading Bloomsbury literary light, but I failed to read either novel; the only novel of Virginia Woolf I have read is *Orlando*, published in 1928, and that I read with pleasure and admiration—but not in the Twenties. The rest were just not for me, then or now. My tastes were and are more robust. For me Virginia Woolf is too intellectual, too subtle and complicated and remote from reality.

I was excited by H. M. Tomlinson's novel, *Gallions Reach,* which came out in 1928 and was much acclaimed, and I have retained my admiration for him down through the years.

I dutifully bought Bernard Shaw's *Intelligent Woman's Guide to Socialism* and the following year, as soon as it was published, the Poet Laureate's *The Testament of Beauty*; the one was a useful work of reference for the self-respecting young socialist I occasionally remembered I was, and the other a pious literary intention; it was a best-seller, and 'everybody' with any cultural pretensions bought it. How widely it was actually read, I wonder. There are the great unread best-sellers. In recent times, I have been told, by a bookseller friend, *Dr. Zhivago* was one. The pages of my own copy of *The Testament of Beauty* are, alas, uncut; though that does not mean I shall never read it, for I admire Robert Bridges. I bought his beautiful anthology, compiled in 1915 and published in 1923. More than twenty years later, in 1946, I find I wrote on the fly-leaf:

> '*Thou shoulds't be living at this hour,*
> *Milton, and enjoying power.*
> *England hath need of thee, and not*
> *Of Leavis and of Eliot.*'

I have long forgotten who H. W. Garrod—whose name appears under the lines—was, or where I came across the lines, but I still strongly endorse the opinion they express.

Another non-fiction work which had a tremendous vogue in 1929 was *The Story of San Michele*, by Axel Munthe, a Swedish physician. It was published in the spring and continued to reprint throughout the year, and all through 1930; I was given the sixteenth impression in October, 1930. It is a strange book, full of bizarre adventures, and it was fashionable to debate whether it was 'true' or not. Which was foolish, for Munthe himself wrote in a Preface to the twelfth impression that 'some of the scenes are laid on the ill-defined borderland between the real and the unreal, the dangerous No Man's Land between fact and fancy', adding that he did not ask for better than not to be believed, for it was all sad enough and bad enough anyhow. The greatest writer of short sensational stories, he declared, was Life, 'But is Life always true?' Well, anyhow, fact or fantasy, or a mixture of both, we liked it, and looking at it again now it seems a book that would stand rereading these forty-odd years later.

But not—for me, anyhow—Ernest Hemingway's novel, *A Farewell to Arms*, which was another best-seller of 1929. It is the love-story of an American soldier and a British nurse in wartime Italy, and was powerful stuff in 1929, with its sex scenes and the Caesarian operation at the end. Like Mottram's novel, *The Spanish Farm*, it was an indictment of the immorality of war in terms of human tragedy, but whereas I had been deeply moved by Mottram's novel I did not get along with Hemingway; I disliked the staccato style of writing, and a quality of male sexual aggressiveness characteristically Hemingway. He was not for me, but he made a tremendous impact on the literary scene at the end of the Twenties and even more in the first half of the Thirties. I had a copy of *A Farewell to Arms* at the time, but the only Hemingway among the fiction in my library now is his novella published in 1952, *The Old Man and the Sea*, for which he was awarded the Nobel Prize. But undoubtedly *A Farewell to Arms* was an important novel, and coming as it did at the end of the Twenties, more than ten years after the end of the War, was the beginning of the 'sobering up' which set in with the spate of serious sociological novels of the early Thirties.

12

The lives we lived

Obviously the lives we lived were infinitely various, determined by social and economic conditions, and by temperament. The life Michael Arlen lived in Mayfair was vastly different from that lived by Virginia Woolf and her set in Bloomsbury; the life I lived in the second half of the Twenties, as an up-and-coming young writer, was remote from that of the 'maids' I was so proud to employ. As with the political opinion polls, it depends whom you talk to what results you get. But just as nowadays 'everybody' watches television, and all kinds and conditions of people go on package holidays abroad, taking in Venice and Salzburg as casually as they once settled for Blackpool or Bournemouth, so in the Twenties there were certain things common to all of us who were young then, if not literally at least generally. We all went dancing, whether we did it at the Savoy or on the Criterion Roof, at the Ham Bone Club or at the Hammersmith Palais de Danse, or the 'pallys' that sprang up everywhere like the discothèques of these days. It was very much part of the life we lived, as watching television is for the majority of people nowadays. And because there was no television we went a great deal to the cinema, always referred to as 'the pictures'. There was 'the wireless' to be sure; it was called 'listening in'; it was with ear-phones, of course, and it was a great novelty and a great wonder, though for a long time there was nothing much to listen-in to except weather forecasts and the weekly half-hour concert or gramophone records from the Marconi station. By 1925 there was Jack Payne and his B.B.C. Dance Orchestra, which was immensely popular, and at the *Daily Mail* Ideal Homes Exhibition that year there were large portable wireless sets, with ear-phones, on display. I had myself no interest in wireless and I did not know anyone who possessed a set. There was no intellectual snobbery involved in this; it was total lack of interest; though no one l knew had a wireless, everyone I knew had a gramophone as naturally as they had a cocktail shaker. These two items were necessities for the life we lived; the wireless was not. But for anyone interested in the first experiments with radio and its development Leslie Baily has a long and informative chapter in his *Scrapbook for the Twenties*.

Dining out was another popular pleasure; if you were well off you dined at 'posh' places like Taglioni's or Quaglino's; if you were an ordinary office worker, or something of the kind, you went to the small French and Italian Soho restaurants, such as Antoine's, where Monsieur, and sometimes Madame, waited on you and you got to know them and went back every time as a friend; or Bertorelli's, where every lady was given a carnation buttonhole done up with fern, and silver paper twisted round the stem. You did not dance at these small Soho restaurants; you went there for little intimate dinners *à deux*, with your young man or your girl, and there was a red-shaded lamp on your table, and surreptitiously, as the meal progressed, you held hands. At 'Bert's' you drank Chianti from the rush-covered flasks; at Antoine's you probably drank a sweet white wine, and Asti spumanti, with its sparkle, you considered every bit as good as champagne. It was rather daring at the end of the meal to have a crême de menthe or a Benedictine. I don't think we drank cocktails at these small restaurants, though at the smart places, of course, we had them in the lounge before we went into the restaurants for the meal; we drank sidecars and white ladies and Manhattans—the latter was a whisky cocktail, and tough. As we grew older and more sophisticated we stuck to dry martinis and ate the green olives speared in them, trotting out the joke about the man who was so glad he didn't like olives, because if he liked them he'd have to eat them and he hated them. We were very fond of the shaggy-dog type of story.

For the smart restaurants, of course, we dressed—white tie and tails for the men—but the joy of the little Soho resaurants was that we could go straight from the office. We went to the Lyons Corner Houses, too, and they were considered rather smart, in a vulgar sort of way, and their bright, noisy cheerfulness, with a loud band, was just the thing for two office girls out on a harmless spree, or the married couple up from the suburbs for a Saturday night's 'binge'. But for the romantic occasion you couldn't beat a little place like Antoine's, with the red-shaded lamp on the little table for two, making it so easy to sit knee-to-knee and for hands eventually to find each other among the coffee cups.

Cinemas, too, the big West End ones, often had restaurants where you could have an inexpensive meal in a dim light, with luxurious deep pile carpet under your feet, and exotic potted palms all round, and the cosy warm cinema smell laving you, soothingly. If you were flush you had fried plaice; if you weren't you contented yourself with sardines-on-toast. It was lovely, anyhow, just to *be* there.

The two great meeting places of the 'Bohemians' of the Twenties were the Fitzroy Tavern, in Soho, and, of course, the Café Royal. People were always saying about the Café Royal that it was not like it had been in the 'old days', but for those of us who had never known it then it was good enough, a place in which you could spend all night, if you wanted to, with a cup of coffee or a glass of beer, and where you could be sure to find someone you knew. After the Second World War it was all different— but so was life itself. Not living in town I was not there very often, but it was a place to go to after the theatre, and it was pleasant, also, to dine on the balcony and look down on to the café and pick out celebrities of the literary and artistic world.

The Fitzroy I was taken to several times, but I was not in

those years a pub person, and I was not at ease in the heat and smoke and noise and crowdedness, and I was too young and immature for the sort of people I met there—hard-drinking, hard-living, and, it seemed to me, rather scruffy. Two remarkable women I met there were Anna Wickham, described to me as an 'imagist poet', and the artist, Nina Hamnett. In Anna Wickham I saw only a lumpish older woman whose conversation I did not understand, and who recited to me what I took to be a line of satiric verse taking a dig at Edith Sitwell—'*It isn't the aspidistra, it's the poet, Edith.*' I was prepared to believe Nina Hamnett was a fine artist—as indeed she was—but to my young eyes she seemed an unattractive and grubby 'Bloomsbury type', though I was assured that in the evenings, when she made an effort, she could look 'mahv'lous'. I made the mistake of putting her, thinly disguised as a sculptress having an affair with a young boxer, into a novel—I forget now which one—and when this was reported to her she declared that next time she saw me she would give me a black eye . . . after which I avoided the Fitzroy.

I was introduced to the Fitzroy by the Irish poet and novelist, Francis Stuart, whose novels won considerable acclaim in the early Thirties. Compton Mackenzie gave high praise to his third novel, *The Coloured Dome*—his first was *Women and God*, but it was by his second, *Pigeon Irish*, that he became known —and for his fourth, *Try the Sky*, wrote a foreword in which he suggested that Francis Stuart had 'a message for the modern world of infinitely greater importance than anything offered by D. H. Lawrence'. As I indicated earlier, we did not shrink from superlatives in those days. What I myself found attractive in Francis Stuart at that time was the combination of dreamy, Celtic romanticism with all of the Irish passion for horse-racing and the Irish capacity for hard drinking. His great friend was Liam O'Flaherty, who was similarly addicted, though the author of *The Informer* was hardly a romantic. In the Twenties and Thirties O'Flaherty was something of a legend, for it was said of him that he had only to turn his intensely blue eyes on a woman for her to fall into his arms. . . . I always wanted to meet him, to prove that it was not necessarily so, but I did not in fact meet him until the Fifties, in Paris, and by that time the legend was not what it had been.

My friendship with Francis Stuart survived the war and into the Fifties; in recent years it has lapsed because I no longer go to Ireland and he no longer comes to London—which in the Twenties and Thirties he loved, as he wrote in his 'Notes for an Autobiography', *Things to Live For*, published in 1934, but, when he wrote, that world was already falling apart.

It is significant that Michael Arlen had his *Green Hat* heroine spend her wedding night with Boy Fenwick in an hotel in Deauville, for at that time there was a craze for Deauville and Dinard; the Belgian resort, Ostend, was also popular, but Deauville was the most fashionable of them all, for some reason, and in all the glossy magazines which depicted the doings of Society there were pictures of the Smart Set disporting themselves on its sands. Le Touquet, south of Boulogne, was also very fashionable. Later in the decade the celebrities moved south into the sun, and Juan-les-Pins became fashionable.

Part of the attraction of these French resorts was the gay life as represented by the casino—you were seen on the *plage* by day and at the casino by night. The most famous of all the French casinos, of course, was at Monte Carlo, but Monte Carlo was not particularly fashionable, though for a time Cannes, with its newly opened casino, had a vogue.

Ostend, I think, was fashionable only to a lesser degree; but still, it was rather dashing to spend a weekend there, and this my husband and I did. We probably settled for Ostend rather than Le Touquet or Deauville because it was cheaper. At Ostend you danced and gambled at the Kursaal—the casino—there was nothing else to do there. In retrospect it seems strange that I should have wished to go to one of those Smart Set casino places, for I had no gambling instinct whatsoever, nor have I now; but crazes are contagious.

We never repeated the experience, and when later I went to Monte Carlo and Cannes the casino did not interest me in the least, and I had not gone because by then the Riviera had become fashionable, but for the sun and palms, orange trees and mimosa, and that exciting feeling of being 'abroad' for which it seemed necessary to go South, the north coast of France, with its grey seas and cloudy skies, being too much like home.

In all the books about the Twenties I have looked at I have found no mention of this craze for the northern French resorts, or of the lure of the casino, which is strange, for it lasted for some years and was very much a feature of the gossip columns of the Press and of the glossy society magazines.

Douglas Goldring in his book about the Twenties makes no mention of Le Touquet and Deauville, but is caustic about the English good-timers in the South of France towards the end of the decade. He refers to the 'physically enchanting but morally enervating Côte d'Azur', listing smart brothels, pornographic cinemas, gambling hells, and 'exclusive' clubs, and the 'glutinous notes' of a song called *My Blue Heaven* pouring out of 'every cheap "dancing", every gramophone, along the Riviera.' He left it early in 1930 to return to an England 'in which all the bright hopes of the early Twenties had been extinguished'.

I am sure Goldring was right in his judgment that a little of the Riviera was a tonic and too much of it a poison, but I was never there long enough to be aware of its viciousness and corruption—though I was strongly aware of this in Majorca in the early Thirties. For me in the Twenties the Côte d'Azur was truly a 'blue heaven', an escape into warm sunshine and bright colour from the endless cold greyness of the English winter. That Suzanne Lenglen was to be seen at Cannes meant nothing to me, but the morning I went down to the *plage* at Juan-les-Pins with Douglas Goldring and his wife and saw Alexandra Danilova, whom I adored as the loveliest of all the Russian ballet dancers, I understood at last the enraptured, reverential, awed, 'Ah, did you once see Shelley plain?' Quite as beautiful she was in the Riviera sunlight as in the limelight. Indeed, blessedly, I saw her plain. I have remembered her as wearing a dark one-piece bathing-suit, and because memory can play one tricks I looked up in my *Confessions* what I wrote at the time, and I have this: '. . . only music can adequately convey the lyric loveliness that is Alexandra Danilova. I once saw her on the sands at Juan-les-Pins. Amongst all those other women with

their pseudo-pearls, their make-up, their bracelets, their coloured costumes, their flaming parasols, little Danilova in her dark
costume, with no make-up, no jewellery, only her pale grave
beauty was like a madonna lily in a field of strident poppies.
For a moment the lovely music of *Les Sylphides* crept up like
an invisible wave of pure beauty on that garish shore.'

I wrote about Ostend in my novel, *Sounding Brass*, making my
advertising man hero—or 'anti-hero'—spend his unromantic
honeymoon there; the chapter is entitled, 'The Kursaal'. He
chose Ostend because it had been suggested to him by a client,
'who had just spent an unofficial honeymoon there, and it was
easy to get to, and when you got tired of Ostend you could go
on to Brussels. Rickard thought that Ostend would do very
well. He had always heard that it was a gay, fashionable sort
of place.' When he got there 'his principal impressions were of
the extreme bareness of the front and the likeness of the Kursaal
to the Albert Hall'. Strolling out on to the balcony of his luxury
hotel he 'studied the Belgian Albert Hall, the striped awnings of
the cafés, and the amazing ugliness of the front, and decided
that the place compared unfavourably with Brighton'.

After dinner he and his dull and unloved bride walk along
the front to the Kursaal, where a concert is in progress, and
'people sat about at little tables drinking wines, beer, or coffee,
according to their nationalities and temperaments'. Mrs.
Rickard observes with satisfaction that 'nearly everyone was in
evening dress, and it was all very decorous, in spite of the drinking'. An old man in uniform slips a footstool under her feet and
a programme into her hand. Rickard is very bored and wonders why they had ever gone in. 'But at ten o'clock the concert
terminated; barely had the last note of the Sonata Pathétique
died away before a saxophone wailed nasally upon air still
quivering with the strings of the violins. Jazz rushed in like a
gust of wind from the real world and swept away the *chanson
triste* of a forgotten age. The air pulsed and vibrated; the erst-
while tense, solemn crowd seemed to give itself a shake of relief
and then broke up into individual units, eager, hurrying units
who formed themselves into a general exodus into the dancing-

room at the other end. They were like children released from
school. . . . On a platform at the far end, a jazz band rocked and
swayed in an ecstasy of rhythm.

> *"When I go to see Hortense,*
> *I always take a pennyworth of pep-per-mints . . ."*

'Men and women who had but a moment before been listening with full hearts, glistening eyes and uncomfortable throats,
to music plaintive with the burden of dead dreams, now paused
but to secure a table by flinging down a handbag or a wrap
upon a seat, and then joined the steadily increasing crowd of
dancers on the shining floor.

> *"She's got no money but she's got sense."*

Beethoven was dead but Jazz was alive.'
Rickard watches the dancers with amusement. 'It was a funny
pastime, he thought, all this jigging around to catchy music.
He noticed a couple dancing in a springy sort of way as though
they were on hot bricks. They let themselves go at the knees and
rocked together rhythmically, with a good deal of "shimmy".
The crowd on the floor was so thick in a few minutes that it
represented nothing so much as a bobbing mass formation.'
Mrs. Rickard observes with shocked disapproval that one of
the girls dancing wears a dress that does not cover her knees,
'and there was another of those awful split skirts'.
But she hankers after a glimpse of the playing-rooms at the
Kursaal—'Just so that one can say one's seen a casino, you
know.'
(Can that be why I had hankered after Le Touquet and
Deauville, and why the trip to Ostend was finally embarked
upon?)
I would not have written it quite like that nowadays; certainly a concert audience would not have had tears in their eyes
and lumps in their throats listening to the Sonata Pathétique,
but it was written from the life and gives, I think, some idea of
the scene.

13

The Diaghileff Ballet

There are people who have written books about the Twenties without mentioning the Diaghileff Ballet; any number of them. I find this very puzzling, because for me all that was silly, trivial, regrettable, and just plain bad in the decade is redeemed by the fact that it was the decade of the Russian Ballet, with wonderful people such as Danilova, Massine, Woizikovski, dancing. They were all fine—Serge Lifar, David Lichine, Anton Dolin (Patrick Kay), Markova—little Alice Marks, the 'miniature Pavlova'—but Alexandra Danilova, Léonide Massine, Leon Woizikovski were the great ones for me, and the ones I have most vividly remembered, and not until the advent of Fonteyn and Nureyev in recent years have there ever been for me any ballet dancers of the stature of those three. I do not assert that they were the greatest; I am not an authority on the ballet; I only say that that is how it has been for me, whose introduction to this great art was in the Twenties.

In those days older people were always saying to us young balletomanes, 'Ah, but you should have seen Nijinsky!' when we raved of Massine and Woizikovski, and 'Ah, but you should have seen Pavlova!' when we were lyrical about Danilova. Now that we have Fonteyn and Nureyev the young are not enjoined to remember the past, I think, for greatness is in our midst again. I was too young for the first Diaghileff seasons before World War I, and even for the return of the Diaghileff Ballet to London, at the Alhambra Theatre, in 1921, with *The Sleeping Princess,* though I was twenty or twenty-one by then; I did not begin to stretch my wings until later in the decade, and then *Les Sylphides* was my first ballet.

Arnold Haskell, who is undoubtedly the supreme authority on ballet, tells us in his book, *Balletomania,** that *The Sleeping Princess* was a failure, and that 'its failure altered the whole course of ballet, kept Diaghileff from London for many years, and made him bitter and disappointed'. Fortunately he came back to us. He took the 1921 production off after 105 performances, at enormous loss, and never revived it in full again. Yet it is the great classical ballet of the Russian Imperial theatre; Tchaikovsky was commissioned to compose the music for it in 1888, and the dress rehearsal took place on January 2, 1890, at the Maryinski Theatre, St. Petersburg, in the presence of the Tsar and the court but was coolly received. The Tsar, Tchaikovsky records in his diary, said that it was 'very nice'; but it found a public, nevertheless, and fired the imagination of the young intelligentsia of the time, amongst whom were Benois, Bakst, and Diaghileff—who was to put it on thirty years later with décor by Bakst. It was done, as *The Sleeping Beauty,* by the Royal Ballet at Sadler's Wells in 1939, with Margot Fonteyn and Robert Helpmann, and with the same dancers at the reopened Royal Opera House in 1946, and has been done many times since, with tremendous success; I did not get to it until 1969, with Fonteyn still as Aurora, but Nureyev now as the Prince.

After the death of Diaghileff in 1929, which was for so many of us the end of an era, Colonel W. de Basil formed Les Ballets Russes de Monte Carlo in 1931 and kept the company together for a few years; when this disbanded I lost interest in ballet; it was no longer *Russian* ballet. I did not get back to ballet until 1966, when, knowing of my great desire to see Nureyev, a friend secured tickets for *Romeo and Juliet,* in which he danced with Fonteyn. This for me was ballet in the great tradition—the Diaghileff tradition. Since then, thanks to this same good friend, I have been able to see Fonteyn and

* 1934.

H

Nureyev in *Swan Lake*, in 1967, *Giselle*—which I missed in the Twenties—in 1968, and then *The Sleeping Beauty* in 1969.

To convey, adequately, the intensity of feeling the young balletomanes of the Twenties brought to bear on the Diaghileff Ballet I cannot do better than quote from what I wrote at the time, in a chapter entitled 'Memories of the Russian Ballet' in my *Confessions*; I wrote shortly after Diaghileff's death in 1929: 'There was nothing like the Russian Ballet for making one feel that one had grown wings and soared amongst the stars. Last-nights were as exciting as *premières*. I have always remembered the spectacle of a young man in the amphitheatre; he had clapped and cheered until he was exhausted; he was leaning over the rail with his long fair hair falling over his face and crying hoarsely, "Serge! Serge!" Serge Lifar was standing in his *Aurora's Wedding* blue velvet and holding a huge wreath of golden laurels. Finally when he could clap and cheer no longer the young man sank back into his seat, huddled there in a state of collapse. But a black-haired Eton-cropped young hermaphrodite standing next to him continued to wave and clap and yell. There was a great cry for Sokolova that night—she had been the Swan princess. The upper circle was still yelling for her long after the safety curtain had descended. "So-ko-lo-va! So-ko-lo-va!" Audiences would call like that for Désormière when he had been conducting, and the upper circle go on calling long after the stalls and dress circle and boxes were out on the pavement looking for their cars. The emotional fervour, the wild hysteria, of those Russian Ballet farewells, the flowers, the wreaths, the exhausting applause, the relentless calling of the gods—to the gods. It was something unique in the theatre.'

I believed then, as many people did, that because Diaghileff was dead and the company disbanded, some of them gone into revue, others into oblivion, such uniqueness would never come again; but I was wrong; it came again with the advent of Margot Fonteyn and Rudolf Nureyev.

Of the ballet first-nights—and the first-night was much more 'the thing' then than I think it is now—I wrote: 'All the interesting oddities of humanity seemed to find their way to the

Russian Ballet; Edith Sitwell in long green brocade with long tight sleeves; Ernest Thesiger thin as a lath and with the look of a vicious ascetic . . . as though *The Little Flowers of St. Francis* and *Fleurs du Mal* might repose side by side amongst his bed-side books. Osbert and Sacheverell Sitwell could always be found at the ballet on a Monday night when the new ballets were presented . . .

'At His Majesty's, at the Lyceum, at Covent Garden, ah, how little we dreamed that Covent Garden would be the swan-song of the ballet, that for the last time we had seen *Aurora's Wedding*, which bored us as a ballet yet which was somehow part of the ritual, like the floral tributes and the hysterical ap-plause from the upper circle. So naïve, that *Aurora's Wedding*, and we knew every note and step of it by heart—a little ridicu-lous, with every artist doing his or her "little piece", but what scope it gave us for letting ourselves go over our favourites, and how some of us resented it when Anton Dolin first took over the blue-bird rôle that had always been little strutting Idzikov-ski's; and how the upper circle nearly fell off its perilous perches with deliriously happy excitement when the "Three Ivans" came whirling on and Woizikovski's wonderful smile flashed out. . . . And how some of us would wait impatiently for the banalities of the fairy-tales to be got through and the arrival of the supreme moment when Danilova and Serge Lifar would dance that final *pas de deux.* . . .

'But the curtain has gone down now for the last time on that concluding pageantry of velvets and brocades and feathers, on the duchesses, the marquesses, the cavaliers, the maids of honour, the Nubian slaves waving their great fans, on the por-celain princesses and the naïve fairy-tale people; no more the stately polonaise, the gay mazurka, no more the rapture of that *pas de deux.* . . . And no more the fire-lit background of the camp of *Prince Igor*, or the exciting simplicities of *The Mid-night Sun* and Rimsky-Korsakoff's unforgettable music. . . . Woizikovski a flame of life as the Midnight Sun, and Danilova a white flame of pure beauty as the Snow Maiden.'

In a sense the *Russian* ballet did die with Diaghileff, though Colonel de Basil kept it alive for a few more years; then came

World War II, and after that it was a different world, a different life.

I believed with Karsavina that the Russian Ballet had reached its limits before Diaghileff died, that it was already pursuing a course which would have led, inevitably, to the ultimate destruction of the artistic form it set out to achieve. I wrote that it had 'passed from the romantic movement of Fokine to the modernities of Massine. Even within the circle of the romantic movement itself it is a long way from *Carnaval* and *Les Sylphides* to *The Fire-bird* and *Petruchka;* and in the new choreography it is a long way from *The Midnight Sun* and *Children's Tales, Le Pas d'Acier* and *Le Sacre du Printemps.* Balanchine with *The Cat, The Bull, The Prodigal Son,* went still farther, and by the time we got to *Renard,* with choreography by young Lifar himself, we know that the ballet had exploded itself. *Renard* was not merely danced, it was sung and played. The night it was produced for the first time in London we had the whole history of the ballet, we had Fokine's *Carnaval,* Nijinsky's *Faune,* Balanchine's *The Gods Go a-Begging*— but it should have been *The Cat,* for in *The Gods Go a-Begging,* with Handel music and Bakst scenery, Balanchine reverted to an earlier mood of the ballet and re-embraced the romantic tradition of Fokine.

'Polemics were inseparable from the Diaghileff ballet, of course—as they must be with any movement essentially occupied with living art—but whether one feels that the ballet has already gone beyond its true aesthetic limits, or whether one perceives it as merely upon the threshold of a new artistic renaissance, the fact remains that it drew to it much that was vital in European art. There was a tendency for anyone who had anything interesting to say in terms of aesthetics to gather round Diaghileff—in painting Picasso, Pruna, Braque, Matisse, Derain, Bakst; in music, Debussy, Satie, Auric, Stravinsky, Sauguet, Rieti, Berners, Poulenc, stand out. This country, France, Germany, Italy, Spain, all brought their contribution of whatever was newest and most interesting. Diaghileff was the rallying point of radical contemporary European art; his genius took each individual unit and gave it coherence and a new form, as part of a whole. Now that he is gone and the ballet disintegrated there is no longer that artistic unity. He achieved so much that what he might or might not have achieved within the next few years melts away as of comparative unimportance. The tragedy of his genius is that his art has not the static quality of painting or sculpture, or musical or literary composition; with the cessation of his directing and controlling ego it, too, ceased to be; the choreographers, the painters, the composers, the dancers, are still there, but disintegrated like so many broken and scattered pieces of a Grecian urn.'

After that last summer season of 1929 at Covent Garden, until Colonel de Basil gathered them all together again, the dancers, choreographers, all who had contributed to the splendid whole that was the Russian Ballet, were disbanded and dispersed, 'a flock without a shepherd'.

But for the entire decade of the Twenties we had this 'true synthesis of the arts', as Haskell defines ballet, and Diaghileff was the high priest of what was in a sense a religion. For we did worship; to the great classical ballets, *Les Sylphides, Swan Lake, L'Après Midi d'un Faune, Le Coq d'Or, Petruchka, Le Boutique Fantasque,* we brought something very like reverence; to the modern ballets we brought—for the most part—the eager excitement and enthusiasm we brought to everything new. We were amused by the Cocteau ballet—with a curtain by Picasso *Le Train Bleu,* in which Anton Dolin danced Le Beau Gosse. No blue train appears in the ballet, and no particular *plage* is indicated, but the dancers in bathing costume satirised the craze for sports and athletics and the Deauville-Riviera cult. In the same mood we liked *Les Matelots,* with music by Georges Auric, choreography by Massine, décor by Georges Braque. Nina Hamnett is said to have whistled English sea-chanties to Auric, which he incorporated into the last of the ballet's five tableaux. As both Lifar and Woizikovski danced in it it satisfied both schools of balletomane taste. *The Triumph of Neptune* in 1926 I dismissed at the time as a 'Sitwell-Berners concoction'; the choreography was by Balanchine; it was 'balletified pantomime', and the purists among us disliked it, but in general it was popular. *Le Pas d'Acier,* with music by Serge Prokofiev and choreography by Massine we who prided ourselves on being 'modern' were really morally bound to like—whether we did or not. We referred to it as the 'factory ballet'; it was a glorification of factory workers and machines, and has been described as 'Diaghileff's one flirtation with Communism'. *Ode*, in 1928, another Massine ballet, we were bound to admire intellectually, or be damned as low-brow, for it was concerned with nothing less than 'metaphysical speculation about Man in the Universe'. *Apollon Musagete,* Stravinsky-Balanchine, was another abstract affair, but was very beautiful, with Serge Lifar, and the female rôles danced by Danilova, Tchernicheva, and Doubrovska.

In 1928, also, we had *The Gods Go a-Begging*, which, though new was not 'modern', with its old Bakst scenery,* and Handel music arranged by Sir Thomas Beecham; it was simple, and beautiful in a classical manner. It was supposed to be a 'rococo impromptu', planned as a compliment to Beecham. Danilova and Woizikovski were the principal dancers, which, for me, with the lovely music, added up to something most wonderful.

Diaghileff's last ballet, *Le Fils Prodigue*, produced in Paris in May, 1929, was another Balanchine ballet, with music by Prokofiev and décor by Georges Raoult. Lifar was the prodigal son and Doubrovska his seducer. It came to London in July, a month before Diaghileff's death, and won Lifar tremendous acclaim—he was to declare later that he would never dance like that again. I did not see it, but Karsavina was critical of it, and as my ideas about ballet were much in line with hers I doubt if I should have liked it. I think the only modern Diaghileff ballet I really liked was *Le Chat*, a Balanchine ballet with music by Henri Sauguet, and lovely thin Alice Nikitina stalking on her points as the cat. It was all in black and white, with costumes and décor in some kind of shiny patent leather.

Well, there were so many, classical old favourites and modernistic novelties, down through the years; I saw most of them, inveterate first-nighter and last-nighter that I was. And in it all was intensely partisan—Woizikovski versus Lifar, Danilova versus Tchernicheva. But despite my partiality for Danilova I

* Bakst died in 1924.

thought Tchernicheva as the nymph in the *Faune* superb, because she had the right quality of mockery, and I could not image Danilova in the role.

But for me Serge Lifar was miscast as the faun. I wrote at the time that he was 'as beautiful as a painting on a Greek vase, but he wasn't a faun; he was never anything but a beautiful boy. When he grasped the little blue garment of the loveliest of the elusive nymphs and carried it away in triumph to the top of the sun-warmed rock, though clasping it to him eagerly, drawing it to himself, as he sank face downwards on the rock and slipped again into his dream-tranced sleep, it was never more than a strip of blue cloth, a veil, a scarf, a piece of material out of a draper's shop. . . . But when Woizikovski bore it away to the rock it was a woman he carried in his arms, a woman he held at arm's length, gazing upon before he drew her to him and slipped down with her in his embrace, in exquisite sensuality, an ecstasy of voluptuousness . . .'

There is more in the same lyrical strain—we let ourselves go in our aesthetic enthusiasms in those days, emotionally naked and unashamed—but it adds nothing except to ask, 'Was Nijinsky better? Can pure beauty be surpassed?'

I should like very much to have seen Nijinsky, but his *Faune* was done in 1912–13, and by 1918 he had been overtaken by schizophrenia and withdrawn from the world of reality.

I do not remember in what year I saw Tamara Karsavina in the dramatic Fokine ballet, *Thamar*, but it was early on, and I did not dream that at the end of the decade I would meet her, not casually but on a basis of friendship. We met whilst I was writing my *Confessions* in 1929, when I lunched with her at her house in Regent's Park, and in due course she came here, with her husband, Henry Bruce, who died in 1951; her letter telling me of this terrible loss was one of the last I received from her; the friendship lapsed some time in the Fifties, I think from lack of sufficient mutual interest to sustain it; very few friendships last a lifetime, because life itself changes, and our interests and activities become differently orientated.

But at the end of the Twenties and in the early Thirties there was the mutual interest in the Ballet, though Diaghileff was already dead by then, and I was her Beautiful Friend and she was the wonderful Karsavina whose name was as much a legend for me as that of Pavlova, whom I never saw.

The first time I set eyes on Karsavina was in *Thamar*, in which she was the voluptuous, cruel and beautiful queen luring young men to a feast of love and death, waving a beckoning rose-red scarf from a high tower, luring travellers to their doom. The ballet is described as a 'choreographic drama in one act'. It was first produced in Paris in 1912, with Karsavina as the queen, and Diaghileff gave her the clue to the interpretation of the rôle in a single sentence—'Omission is the essence of Art— eyebrows in a single line.' Haskell says that the 'ballet of the emotional subject is always dangerous. Karsavina made it possible'.

I saw *Thamar* only once, but it made a profound impression on me. Years later I saw Karsavina again not in ballet but at a big dinner at Stationers' Hall; I have forgotten what was the occasion, or who was my escort, but it was evidently a very dull affair, with women in the minority, and a number of long and tedious speeches; then suddenly across the room I saw a strikingly beautiful woman and inquired who she was and was told she was Thamar Karsavina. 'The name fell like music into the droning dreariness', I recorded. 'Memory wakened and became a flame. The steady rise and fall of the beckoning scarf . . .'

I must have written to her after that asking if I could meet her and include her in the Impressions part of *Confessions and Impressions*, for I have a letter from her in which she suggests that I would get the best impression of her by seeing her in her own surroundings, and saying that if I could lunch with her 'on a Wednesday' she would be 'overjoyed'. She signed that letter —all her letters were written in her big scrawling hand—Thamar Karsavina; as the friendship developed she became, simply, 'Tamara'.* On the pretty, old-fashioned Valentine she gave me on that first visit in February she wrote, 'a Valentine from one who wishes to be your friend'. I still have it, and the photograph of herself in 1924, which she gave me in 1931, and on which

* This was her husband's preferred version of her name, and is the one she herself prefers. To Diaghileff she was always Thamar.

she wrote : 'To Ethel, with love and admiration, Thamar.' She gave me, also, a copy of her book, *Theatre Street*, which came out in March, 1930, inscribed, 'To Ethel Mannin with my fond love, Thamar, 1930.'

I think I cannot do better than quote from my chapter on her in the *Confessions*, which I called a Portrait in Pastel :

'I was glad there was snow on that day when I first came to her house, for the white trees at every window converted Regent's Park into a Russian landscape and made it easy for her to talk of Petrograd. The mysterious silence of falling snow, and Karsavina in her low voice, with its rhythmic accent, talking of St. Petersburg before the Revolution, with its baroque palaces, the classic austerity of its public buildings, its wooden houses, such love in her voice, and all the wistfulness of the exile. She was months getting out of Russia, but she did not fare badly at the hands of the Bolsheviks; they had, she said, a contempt for the intelligentsia, but a profound respect for the artist. As an artist she might remain in the country without suffering personal harm, or leave it without let or hindrance. Some of the possessions she left behind came back to her in England—she bought them back. She saw a carpet in a shop window in a Regent Street stores and recognised it as her own; she went into the shop and asked them where they had procured the carpet; they told her from Soviet Russia; she told them she could give them the design in detail—it was of special design and hand-woven—and the stores sold it back to her at the price they had paid for it. She recovered several chandeliers in the same ironic manner—by buying them back; but she was much too overjoyed to have them back to feel any bitterness about it.

'Her house is completely expressive of her personality. Pale pink walls, pastel blue ceilings, baroque gilt scrolls, stone angels, a gilt St. Florian over a marble mantelpiece, Louis Quinze chairs, superb chandeliers, a hanging blue glass star; shelves of Russian china, formal flower prints on the pink or yellow walls, and sketches of ballet costumes she has worn, crowding books, English, French, German, little deliberate touches of theatricality expressed in a drift of red silk draped over a stone carv-

ing above a mantelpiece, and in endless little charming artifici-
alities. A gay, coloured, completely theatrical atmosphere,
eclectic as Karsavina herself. A touch of the baroque, more
than a touch of the rococo—but a charming rococo, like that
of the Chauve Souris. . . . And to know Karsavina is to find it
impossible to visualise her in any other setting. She has an
intellectual admiration of the modern school of interior decoration, but it omits that element of the frankly theatrical
which is emotionally important to her, so that she can admire
without liking it, as she does the music of Stravinsky. Her personality is essentially of the theatre—yet she is completely without affectation, and utterly sincere. But she loves the theatre, the
colour and pulse and flavour of it, and has done since she was
a child. She has a doll's house furnished in the same manner as
her own house, with the same touches of gilt and wine-coloured
silk and formal decorativeness, and a tiny doll in a stiff pink
silk gown lying in an ornate little French bed. Yet from delighted contemplation of the doll's house she will look up and
speak of the essays of Lamb, or the novels of Dostoievski.

'She has a great love of the English language and the arrangement of words. She reads Lamb over and over again for sheer
delight in his purity of style. Two contemporary novels which
delighted her more than anything she had read recently were
Harriet Hume and *The Bridge of San Luis Rey*, and she la-
mented that *A Mirror for Witches* was not better known. We
talk of modern novels for a while, and then she takes from a
shelf a book of German fairy-tales and explains from the illustrations their scope for ballet. She is planning to do some of
them for a short season in Germany in the autumn. There is no
place for ballet in this country any more, she sighs, "unless one
is content to be a music-hall turn".

'Her admiration for Diaghileff is boundless, but she felt that
even before his death the Russian Ballet was nearing its end,
because, she insisted, it had reached its limits and tried to go
beyond, and any great art must finish when it tries to do that.
"When dancing develops into acrobatics that is the end of dancing as ballet," she said, and for a few minutes we mourned the
prospect of a superb artist like Woizikovski being reduced to

touring the provinces and the suburbs with all the glory of the ballet behind him . . . Woizikovski, the greatest artist of them all, an echo of Nijinsky himself. Could nothing be done? Did no one care?'

(Well, someone was to care, Colonel de Basil, but that was not until 1931, and we were talking when Diaghileff was newly dead.)

'In Thamar Karsavina's philosophy of life there is a pattern and a rhythm, to deviate from which involves discord and disintegration; one must work out one's destiny, not seek to resist it . . . For her how should life be other than the working out of a geometric pattern, a choreographic rhythm?

'When she gave me the Valentine she said, "Now we must be friends for a year!" '

I concluded my piece about her with words which I still think true: There is only one person more memorable than *Thamar* of the ballet, and that is Thamar Karsavina herself.

She wrote thanking me for the pleasure my visit had given her, saying that she felt happy in my presence, and she had been deeply touched, she wrote, by the gift of the pink azalea in a gilt pot I had sent her to express my thanks for the afternoon I spent with her. She liked very much what I wrote about her—which I showed her before publication—but asked me as a favour to modify something I had written about Lifar and Pavlova; I have no idea, now, what it was, but whatever it was I deleted it entire, for there is no reference to either in this Karsavina chapter.

When she wrote to me on January 7, 1930, she was rehearsing at the Lyric, still planning to find time to come to Oak Cottage, and was going to telephone Woizikovsky and tell him what I had written about him (this would have been what I wrote in the chapter about herself, for the book was not published until June, and I had not sent her the whole Ballet chapter) adding that he was not only 'a wonderful dancer but ever such a nice upright boy'. Soon after that she came to Oak Cottage with her very likable husband. When she wrote in 1952 she did so from Hampstead and her husband was dead. She urged me to telephone her and arrange a meeting, but I was to-ing and fro-ing a good deal between England and Ireland at that time—I had the cottage in Connemara until 1963—and one way and another it 'didn't work out'. I thought then my attempt to revive the friendship had come too late, though she said that it was 'never too late'—that the heyday of the friendship was over, that it belonged to an era that finished, really, with the death of Diaghileff, but when I visited her, nearly forty years later, in her beautiful seventeenth-century house in Hampstead, to which she moved with her husband in the Fifties. I did not find her so very much changed, and certainly not looking her age. But I had forgotten how small she is, and the deep, warm timbre of her voice. That her thick lovely hair should now be grey was, of course, to be expected, and that there should be some lines in her face—though in fact she has fewer than many women much younger; but the fine dark eyes are still bright, and her skin stretched smoothly on the high cheekbones is clear. In her eighties Thamar Karsavina is still a classically beautiful woman. She carries herself straightly, still, in spite of severe arthritis which makes walking laborious for her, and when she is seated, sitting bolt upright, her ankles crossed, slender feet in pointed soft slippers, suddenly one is aware of the beautiful dancer's legs, the unconscious ballerina grace, of her attitude. She is still intellectually alert and emotionally alive, still intensely interested in Ballet, that *Theatre Street*, which was and is her life; and when, on and off, she realises her age, she told me, she is astonished by it, since she is herself unchanged.

I had written to her, after the monstrous lapse of time, as a 'voice from the past', and she replied that that voice 'brought back the warm friendship of those days', adding that she believed that 'nothing of value ever dies with age, and so it is of our friendship'. Certainly it is true of Thamar Karsavina herself; she is the incarnation of the immortal truth that 'A thing of beauty is a joy forever; Its loveliness increases; it will never pass into nothingness. . . .'

PART III

The end of an Era

14

Overflow to the Thirties

The Twenties overflowed into the Thirties; you cannot take
any decade and draw hard and fast lines as to its beginning and
its end; the 'Twenties' as a period of social history began before
January 1, 1920; the era began somewhere in 1918 with the
post-war mood, and it ended somewhere around 1936, with the
Spanish Civil War and intimations of evil yet to come. The
Twenties 'mood' continued into the early Thirties, and at the
end of 1929 there was no general realisation of the impending
economic Depression. It has been said that the Twenties had
the 'unique distinction of being the most deflationary period in
English history since the Black Death in 1348. The cost of living
dropped, and life was more interesting and varied than ever before. Despite the industrial troubles and the unemployment
many looked back, in the dark years that lay ahead, to a golden
age.'*

Diaghileff died on August 19, 1929; D. H. Lawrence on
March 2, 1930; their deaths were felt as very great losses to
those of us who were young in the Twenties; but the Diaghileff
Ballet had already reached its peak and entered its decline into
acrobatics before Diaghileff's death; and it is difficult to see
where Lawrence could have gone after *Lady Chatterley's Lover*
and *The Man Who Died*—well, we know where he did go,
which was into what Hugh Kingsmill† called the 'morass' of the

* Richard Bennett in *A Picture of the Twenties*, 1961.
† *D. H. Lawrence*, 1938.

Apocalypse, on which he worked to the end, and which was anti-Christian and anti-democracy, all his latent Fascism breaking through.

At the time we did not see this—Hugh Kingsmill did not write his book about Lawrence until 1938—and in spite of Mussolini we did not really become aware of Fascism until Hitler became Chancellor in 1933. Diaghileff we mourned until *Les Ballets Russes de Monte Carlo* were formed under the direction of Colonel W. de Basil, with lovely and exciting new young *ballerinas*, Baronova, Riabouchinska, Toumanova, and then we knew that Russian Ballet had not died with Diaghileff after all. We did not love Danilova less—I, anyhow, did not—because we took these three brilliant newcomers to our balletomane hearts, nor think less highly of Lifar because there now emerged young David Lichine. There were still the old favourites, the great ones, Woizikovski, Massine, Dolin, Lifar, but there were also these exciting newcomers; you could still see Massine in *Le Beau Danube* with Danilova, ravishing our hearts as always, but you could see him also now with lovely little Irina Baronova, and quite different but fascinating Tatiana Riabouchinska; without feeling unfaithful to Danilova I loved them both . . . though Riabouchinska did not part her hair in the middle in the classical style. Tamara Toumanova in *Les Sylphides* had echoes of Danilova, I thought—a similar sad sweetness; so little and young she was, only about fifteen.

In the summer of 1933 the de Basil company came to London, to the Alhambra, with all the old favourites and the exciting newcomers, and we who had thought that ballet would never be the same again without Diaghileff were won over. De Basil gave us two splendid new ballets: *Choreatium*, which is Brahms' 4th Symphony interpreted in ballet, and *Les Presages,* which is Tchaikovsky's 5th. They were Massine's creations, and Haskell says that with them a fresh period started in the Ballet and in Massine's evolution. *Choreatium* had neither theme nor story; it was purely interpretation, and profoundly beautiful, 'the maximum exploitation of physical beauty in motion', to use another of Haskell's definitions of the Ballet. *Les Presages* is really allegory, Man's struggle with his destiny; evil is repre-

(above) Author and daughter take off for Paris by flying-machine from Croydon, 1925

LAUNCHINGS

(below) Godfrey Winn launches his third novel, *The Unequal Conflict*, with a cocktail party at Ebury Street, 1930. Left to right: Godfrey Winn, Kate Mary Bruce (niece of Somerset Maugham), the author, Lady Patricia Moore, Viscountess Tredegas, Louis Golding, and, behind, Eddie (Sir Edward) Marsh. One of the famous Quaglino brothers christens the book

'Mrs. Lins', who founded Summerhill
School with A. S. Neill at Lyme Regis in
1924, and whom he married in 1927

A. S. Neill at Summerhill, 1925

sented by war and its angry passions; the women try to restrain the men; Man triumphs over the evil spirit of war and all is happiness. David Lichine danced in both these ballets with tremendous success; he had tremendous vitality, and strong personality. We liked him, I think, in the same way that we liked Woizikovski and Massine—for the same reasons.

Perhaps I have written too much about the Ballet, but it was intensely important to me, throughout the Twenties and in those first years of the Thirties which were an extension of the Twenties. There was a wonderful Jubilee Season at Covent Garden in 1935—it was no longer the Monte Carlo Ballet after it reached London, at the Alhambra, but Colonel W. de Basil's Ballets Russes, simply—there were the old Diaghileff favourites, *Les Sylphides, Petrouchka, The Good Humoured Ladies, Le Beau Danube, Swan Lake*, oh, and the *Faune*, and *The Fire Bird*, and *Thamar*—all of them, and the exciting new ones, the Massine ballets, and inevitably, *Aurora's Wedding*. For me, I think for many of us, it was the tremendous finale of the Russian Ballet. There was still ballet, but not Russian Ballet; and over Europe the sky was darkening. Not only over Europe; an African country called Abyssinia began to appear in the headlines, and in October, 1935, there was the Italian invasion and the war was on. The talk was all of 'sanctions' against Italy, and there was the dread of what such a policy might lead to—the first fears of a second world war. There was a luncheon party at Oak Cottage at which we talked of little else; James Hilton was there; I had liked his novel, *Lost Horizon*, very much, and I liked him. I had met Reginald Reynolds in July and he also was there. I was very frightened by all the talk of the possibility of a second world war, and when he was leaving James Hilton laid a hand on my shoulder. 'Don't worry,' he said, 'there isn't going to be a war.' I learned afterwards that he had only said it to comfort me. Soon afterwards he went to Hollywood and we none of us ever saw him again; he died there.

But in Paris Colonel de Basil was training children between seven and twelve, with the great Russian dancers who had settled there, for the Ballet of 1940. It was an act of faith still possible in 1935, *malgré tout*.

I

At the beginning of the decade, however, the mood was not one of enjoying things *malgré tout* : there was, on the contrary, an overflow of euphoria from the Twenties. In the theatre there was Rudolf Besier's *The Barretts of Wimpole Street*, and in the cinema the excitement of Greta Garbo's first 'talkie', Eugene O'Neill's powerful *Anna Christie*, which proved, said the critic, John Bainbridge, that 'Garbo talking was an even more magical figure than Garbo mute'. Arnold Bennett published his novel, *Imperial Palace,* and Vicki Baum her *Grand Hotel,* filmed in 1932 with Garbo. In 1931 there were three romantic musicals in the theatre: *White Horse Inn*—as popular then as *The Sound of Music* in our own time—*Waltzes from Vienna,* Richard Tauber's *The Land of Smiles.* There was also a charming romantic play called *Autumn Crocus,* by Dodie Smith, with Fay Compton as the English spinster who meets the attractive young Austrian in the Tyrol when the autumn crocus is in bloom on the mountain side; the young man was played by Franz—later Francis—Lederer, who wore *Lederhosen* and was good-looking enough to melt any susceptible female heart. Later there was a charming film with Fay Compton repeating her role and with Ivor Novello in the Lederer part.

There was also, to be sure, Noël Coward's quite embarrassingly patriotic *Cavalcade* in the same year, to call us to order, and in 1935 there was the Auden and Isherwood play, *The Dog beneath the Skin,* produced by Rupert Doone, an ex-Diaghileff dancer and choreographer. '*Dog-Skin*', as Isherwood liked to refer to it, was tremendously 'new'—*avant-garde,* as we should say nowadays. It was satire on the Thirties scene; it was clever, it was audacious, and highly original. It was politically conscious, and by the mid-Thirties we were beginning to be that. The young squire hides himself in a dog's skin and has a dog's-eye view of his fellow-man and finds it 'an awful shock to start seeing people from underneath'. He had had no idea that 'such obscene, cruel, hypocritical, mean, vulgar creatures' had ever existed in the history of the planet.

As far back as 1923 we had had the anti-war play of the Capek brothers, *The Insect Play,* with John Gielgud as the tramp; I did not see it then—it was not then the 'must' it had become by 1936, when it was done again in London; its message by then was urgent, and Nancy Price, who put it on as one of her People's Theatre productions, inveigled me into making a speech in front of the curtain, at the end of matinée performances, urging people to take its anti-war message to heart and refuse to be drawn into another war.

In the cinema the great excitements were Charlie Chaplin's *City Lights*, René Clair's *Le Million*, and the Emil Jannings/Marlene Dietrich film, *The Blue Angel*. This last really did 'send' us, as we say nowadays, and it established the sound film, the 'talkie', as nothing else, not even *Show Boat*, had. We had heard Garbo's deep voice, but the point about Dietrich—apart from her sexiness—was that she *sang*, and in a way that was new to us, husky, gravelly, sexy—sexier than anything we'd yet known. Looking back it seems very strange now that there should have been so much resistance to sound films, but Pirandello in 1928 declared that the cinema was digging its own grave, and A. P. Herbert in 1929 prophesied that the 'talkie' was 'doomed to an early but expensive death'. Paul Rotha wrote in his book, *The Film Till Now*, 1930, that 'as a mechanical invention, the dialogue film is doubtless marvellous, and by the aid of clever showmanship is successful in catching the temporary attention of the masses. Nevertheless, all dialogue films are simply reductions to absurdity of the attempt to join two separate arts which, by their essential nature, defy synchronisation. Employed judiciously as a *sound* adjunct to the visual image, the microphone will add value to the camera, but as a means of "realism" its place is non-existent.' But William Hunter, in his book, *Scrutiny of Cinema*, wrote in 1932 : 'Sound is unlimited. The cinema has doubled its potentialities by the acquisition of this new weapon.' There had been some very fine silent films in the Twenties, but whatever the highbrow attitude, and the die-hard attitude of conserving the old 'art form' of the cinema, the vast mass of ordinary people infinitely preferred the sound film, and with its advent a whole new world of entertainment—of art, even—was opened up. 'Glorious Technicolor' was still some way off, but soon after the exciting innovation of sound we had Walt Disney's first colour cartoon, *Flowers and Trees,* and we were on the way to something more exciting still. There was not the critical opposition to colour there had been to sound, despite the fact that the colour was fairly crude, but it was the intellectual thing to prefer black-and-white, as the superior 'art form'—an attitude which survives, I think, to this day. I am a colour addict myself; so far as I am concerned colour and the broad screen have added a tremendous new dimension to what back in the Twenties and Thirties we called, simply, 'the pictures'.

We had some fine films in the first half of the Thirties. We had the German film, *Mädchen in Uniform,* the great Chaplin film—perhaps his greatest—*City Lights,* the great Garbo films, *Anna Karenina, Queen Christina,* and Maugham's *The Painted Veil* . . . these all came after her first 'talkie' in 1930.

We had Elizabeth Bergner in *Der Traümende Mund,* and Conrad Veidt—whom we adored—in *Rasputin,* and Françoise Rosay—whom we also adored—in *La Kermesse Héroïque.* And all the Jean Gabin films. Heavens, how we loved that man, with his cigarette dangling from his lower lip, his curious, subtle charisma, and the doom that invariably hung over him in any situation. He couldn't win; he wasn't meant to; if the police were after him they would eventually get him; if he was trying to reach a ship it would sail without him; if a woman loved him parting was inevitable, and through it all he would saunter with his shabby, nonchalant charm, very French, very much of Marseilles, of the waterfront; there was *Pépé le Moko* in 1936, and at the end of the decade *Quai des Brumes* and *Le Jour se Lève,* black and white, and unimaginable in colour; they were too intensely personal in their drama, and no embellishment was called for.

Of a quite different order in French films—Jean Gabin was anyhow unique—was a lovely Duvivier production in 1933, *Poil de Carotte,* the redhead being a charming freckled little boy, Robert Lynen, who was born in France in 1921 to parents of American origin. He was the appealing little boy to end appealing little boys, and he went straight to our hearts. Whether it was all sentimentality or not I cannot now remem-

ber, but only that we all saw it and loved it and discussed it—
and some of us have remembered it.

The history of this film is interesting. It was based on a novel
by a French author, Jules Renard, who died in 1910, at the
age of forty-six. *Poil de Carotte* was his first novel, and was
dramatised in 1900. A silent film was made by Duvivier in
1925, and the sound version in 1933. Following Robert Lynen's
success as the boy in this film Duvivier gave him a part in *La
Belle Equipe* in 1936, and in that lovely film, *Carnet du Bal*
in 1937. He was in two more films, *La Vie Magnifique* in 1939,
and in *Cap au Large* in 1942. In 1943 he played his last and
finest rôle—in the *maquis*. He was caught by the Germans and
imprisoned in a fortress in Karlsruhe and shot in 1944. By then
the little freckled boy of *Poil de Carotte* would have been
twenty-three.

We had, I think, more of interest in the cinema than on the stage
in those years, though we had the Emlyn Williams play, *Night
Must Fall*, Priestley's *Dangerous Corner*, and Denis Johnston's
The Moon in the Yellow River, of those we 'all' saw and talked
about.

There was also, of course, T. S. Eliot's *Murder in the Cathedral*, which was highly acclaimed by the intelligentsia, but I
early became allergic to T. S. Eliot, and the allergy has per-
sisted to the present day.

There was much else of importance, to be sure, but I am
here primarily concerned with what I personally saw and have
remembered.

It is therefore necessary to say something about the inimitable
Ruth Draper, who first appeared in London in 1916, but I did
not see her until late in the Twenties, and after that whenever
she was in London, which she was, on and off, right up to the
time of her death, at the age of seventy-two, in 1956. Her mono-
logues were so astonishing that although she was always alone
on the stage the characters she brought to life seemed like a
supporting cast. She had a tremendous vogue in the Twenties
and Thirties; she went on right into the Fifties, internationally
famous and with a great following, but in the Twenties and

Thirties she was so splendidly new to us; we were fascinated by her, and her lifelike English Lady Showing the Garden made such an impression on us as to inhibit us when showing our gardens, so that we would say, self-consciously, 'I don't want to do a Ruth Draper on you, but of course the first flush of roses is over now,' or whatever it was we wished the visitor could have seen. If we said it now I think only the older generation would recognise the allusion. We stopped saying it, I think, after her death. On her programmes there was always reproduced the pencil drawing Sargeant made of her.

There was a sobering up in the Thirties, but it found expression more in literature, I think, than in the cinema and theatre; true we had two very important serious films, *All Quiet on the Western Front* and *Journey's End,* and in the theatre Shaw's play, *The Apple Cart*—which was not really a play at all, but only a conversation piece—but they were hangovers from the Twenties—*The Apple Cart* was, in fact, first produced at Malvern in 1929. I saw it in London in 1930, but it was not for me —but then I was never a Shavian.

15

The sobering-up

By the end of the Twenties there were a million more women than men in England; and women were allowed to vote at the age of twenty-one instead of thirty as hitherto—the Equal Franchise Bill of 1928 was passed on the day of the funeral of the great suffragist, Mrs. Emmeline Pankhurst. The 'Flappers' Vote', as it was called, put five million more women on the electoral roll and helped to create the second Labour Government in 1929. Whether I voted at that time I cannot now remember, but probably not; I was probably still too busy living, being at that time newly emancipated from marriage into independence. The election was fought on the issue of unemployment; it was the beginning of the sobering-up after the post-war fling of almost a decade.

The new decade opened with a million-and-a-half unemployed and ended with two and a half millions. In October there was the crash of the world's largest airship, the R101, on its maiden voyage to India, with only six survivors from the fifty-four people on board. It was the end of what in the Twenties had seemed an exciting British dream of the development of airships. The R101 had been launched in October, 1929, and the sister ship, R100, had successfully flown to Montreal and back in the summer of 1930. It was said that the R101 had been launched precipitately following that success, in the British bid for supremacy in this form of aviation. As I have recorded in my *Confessions* I saw the R100 'roaring against the pale blue silk of an early springtide sky, and thought how in its brutal hideousness and terrifying monstrosity it was a symbol of what we have made of civilisation'.

The R101 disaster was a fearful national shock; the sister ship, R100, was broken up, and it was the end of the great airship dream. I was too young in 1912 to remember the shock of the *Titanic* disaster, to which it was likened, but I remember the R101 horror—which was perpetuated for me in a curious fashion, because after it, and right up to the outbreak of the Second World War, I received every time I published a book a foul anonymous postcard signed R101. I could only assume that the writer was mentally ill and that the airship disaster had made some dreadful impact on a sick mind. When I joined the Independent Labour Party in 1933 the motives for my doing so attributed to me on one of these postcards were as monstrous as they were obscene.

Joining the I.L.P. was my own personal sobering-up, but I was still first-nighting and dancing in the first years of the Thirties, though to a lesser extent than in the Twenties. I had formed a friendship with Paul Tanqueray, who was making a name for himself with his portraits of authors, theatrical personalities, and socialites, and the friendship has been maintained to the present day, with unchanging devotion. We went to the first-night of plays and the de Basil ballets together; we went dancing together; I went to his parties, he came to mine; sometimes we met each other at other people's parties—the early Thirties were an extension of the Twenties; the era was expiring, but it was not yet time to say goodbye-to-all-that.

It has its significance, however, that Paul and I went together to a special showing of *Battleship Potemkin* early in the Thirties, in aid of the American Negroes who became known as the Scottsboro Boys, who were arrested in 1931 on charges of the rape of two white girls on a freight train. The long-drawn-out case, with its overtones of racialism, became notorious and attracted a good deal of interest among the intelligentsia here. The special showing of the film, to raise money for the defence, was arranged by Nancy Cunard, who was a staunch defender of the Negroes, and, indeed, all causes involving freedom and justice. I knew her only slightly, and admired her courage—and her looks—whilst not always agreeing with her politically. Paul tells me that he remembers meeting and talking with her on that *Potemkin* occasion.

After that first photograph Paul took of me, in September, 1930, I was never photographed by anyone else. In those days authors' faces did not enliven the dust-covers of their books as frequently as nowadays, and the first Paul Tanqueray picture of me to be used in this way was that first one, which was used on the back of the jacket of the American edition of *Venetian Blinds*—a novel of working-class life in South London as I knew it and lived it before the First World War—in 1933. The 'jazz' background of the photograph was specially designed by Ida Davies, and was considered very 'modern'. Paul still thinks it one of six best photographs. It depicts the author looking— deceptively—sweet and grave. The art of portrait photography in the Twenties and early Thirties was to make the sitter appear as attractive and charming as possible—the gruesome business of 'character' portraiture was still some way off. The early Tanqueray photographs appeared in the Press in connection with the numerous articles I wrote, and in the glossy magazines, and to this day Paul's pictures appear on the jackets of my books.

We were a mutual admiration society, and for the Paul Tanqueray Exhibition of photographs towards the end of 1930 I wrote the introduction to the catalogue; in it I declared, recklessly, that what Picasso was to painting Paul Tanqueray was to the art of photography—which was carrying it a bit far even allowing for the panache of the period. But such fine flourishes were part of the 'scene', like pink ostrich feathers and other pleasant absurdities.

Some time towards the end of the Twenties, before I met Paul Tanqueray, I was photographed by the fashionable and distinguished photographer, E. O. Hoppé. Whether I had the

temerity to approach him, or whether I was sent to him by one
of the glossy publications for which I wrote at that time, I cannot now remember, but it was certainly not a complimentary
sitting, for not only did the photographer who had made portraits of George V and Queen Mary, and who was a personal
friend of Marie of Roumania, and who had photographed
such celebrities as Bernard Shaw, Henry James, Thomas
Hardy, Rabindrinath Tagore, Jacob Epstein, and such lovely
women as Lady Lavery, Anna May Wong, Thamar Karsavina,
have no need to canvass sittings, but in his book, *Hundred Thousand Exposures*, published in 1945, with an introduction by
Cecil Beaton, he speaks very strongly against what he calls the
'pernicious racket' of the 'free sitting'. Whatever the circumstances in which I went to him he made a very attractive picture
of the young woman I was then.

Paul Tanqueray considers E. O. Hoppé the doyen of
British photographers, and the 'forerunner of Beaton'. Cecil
Beaton himself, in his introduction to Hoppé's book—one of a
score—says that the Master, as he called him, did not take photographs of 'anybody', and that his studio was extremely exclusive, 'reserved for portraying the glorious adult world of
art, literature, ballet and of dazzling society'. He wrote of him
as an 'artist in portraiture', and as being 'at home anywhere
throughout the world'. Looking now, so late in the day, at the
wonderful photographs in his book, and at the index, dazzling
with great names, I think I should have felt flattered to have
been accepted as a sitter to the great man, but I do not remember that I did, and I doubt if I did, for I was young-and-twenty, confidently on the way up, and with no more respect for my
elders than the youth of any generation has.

In *Another Window Seat*, the second volume of his autobiography,* R. H. Mottram speaks of the 'inflated promises and
doctrinaire plans of the nineteen-Twenties, that were so thoroughly exploded in the nineteen-Thirties. In 1931 Britain
went off the Gold Standard and government home policy was
to economise on the national housekeeping. There was, as

* 1957.

Mottram puts it, a 'sudden and brutal deflation'. Significantly, in 1932 the Oxford Union carried the motion that 'in socialism lies the only solution to the problems facing this country'. The young intelligentsia began to turn away from the evidently decaying capitalism of the West and look with a wistful eye on the hopeful red dawn of the U.S.S.R. Pilgrimages to Russia, in quest of the far, far better thing, began to be fashionable, along with Russian films shown by film societies and clubs, and it was all taken very, very seriously. The visit to Russia was a kind of baptism into seriousness, the outward and visible sign of having finished with the Twenties and their overflow into the Thirties. I did not make the pilgrimage myself until 1934; I still had some living to do in the overflow.

In January, 1930, I published my Channel Islands novel, *Children of the Earth*, which was done into German and French, and in June my *Confessions and Impressions* were published; both books were written in 1929, but the *Confessions* was not completed until the beginning of the new decade.

From then I began what was to be the regular rhythm of my literary output, more or less sustained to the present day, a novel and a non-fiction book—or in the Thirties sometimes collections of short stories—a year. The novel in January, 1931, was *Ragged Banners*, recklessly dedicated to 'the valiant undefeatable defeated', and with its homosexual overtones was considered daring. It has followed me down through the years as relentlessly and as wearisomely as the *Confessions*. 'Surely,' I have heard myself saying, over and over again, 'the world has moved on since that bit of early work was produced!' Invariably the answer has been, wistfully, 'All the same I liked it!' The speaker has usually been homosexual. Nothing wrong with that, and the loyalty to a book one has once enjoyed, no matter how dated it has become, is something I can understand and appreciate, but though as late as 1938 I defended the novel, in later years I have come to consider it flamboyant and overwritten, and would like it forgotten.

In June, 1931, I published *Commonsense and the Child*, my first non-fiction—other than the *Confessions*—for which

A. S. Neill wrote the preface, in which he said that 'some of your public may revise their opinions of Ethel the novelist and spurn the books of a woman who disbelieves in original sin'— which has a pleasant old-world ring to it now, but at the time Neill's ideas about child education and child psychology were as new as Rousseau's were in his day.

This foray into the field of freedom-for-the-child was followed by a novel about a child, *Linda Shawn*, in 1932; it was dedicated to the composer, Vivian Ellis, whom I had known in the Twenties, and who had always said I should write it, and to my childhood memories of 'Shawn's', which was based on my grandfather's farm. I have always thought that my better work began with that novel.

I was doing a good deal of work for the glossy magazine, *The Bystander*, short stories, parodies of A. A. Milne's Christopher Robin poems, and a weekly social gossip letter from Paris, which some of my more ribald friends referred to as my French letter. . . .

I met Daphne du Maurier through Comyns Beaumont in the spring of 1932; she gave me a copy of her newly published second novel, *I'll Never be Young Again*, about young lovers in Paris in the Twenties, writing in it: 'For Charlotte, this book which is my *Ragged Banners*.' She called me Charlotte because she insisted that I was like Charlotte Brontë as depicted in the famous drawing of her by George Richmond, in the National Portrait Gallery. But beyond the fact that Charlotte Brontë parted her hair in the middle I could never see the likeness; however, Charlotte I was for her and Charlotte I remained, even when we met some twenty years later at some literary occasion, at which many of us in the world of books who had been young in the Twenties, reappeared—ghosts, it seemed to me, from a world that had ended long ago. Not that there was anything ghost-like about Daphne du Maurier; she had been a very attractive girl, and she was in middle age a very beautiful woman. I have two photographs of her, both of which she gave me in the spring of 1932 : one is the charming studio portrait of her reproduced in this book, and which is how

I remember her at that time; the other is a snapshot of her aboard her yacht, and shows her with slacks tucked into wellingtons, her short hair blowing across her face, and is inscribed on the back, in the red ink she always affected, 'Daphne as a boy'—though in point of fact she looks more boyish in the studio portrait. The friendship, which had started off so promisingly, was short-lived—our ways lay apart. I went back to Paris shortly after we met, and she married the man she had described to me as the 'youngest major in the Guards', 'Boy' Browning.* Although I had published a dozen books by the time we met, and she was only in her twenties and had just published her second novel, she quickly outstripped me along the road to literary success—*Jamaica Inn*, in 1936, established her as a best-seller. But it was a happy brief encounter at the outset of her career, and those youthful days when she was 'Dafnee', and I was 'Charlotte' are something to remember with a smile that is perhaps a little wistful, for certainly we'll never be young again. . . .

I had been living and working in Majorca in the spring of 1932 and had hated it, despite its beauty. As I wrote in my second volume of autobiography, *Privileged Spectator*, published in 1938, 'it was infested by every kind of foreign undesirable, drug addicts, dipsomaniacs, crooks, idle rich, and every kind of parasite. There were too many bars and too much drinking; it might have been Montparnasse.' I finished a book of travel sketches, *All Experience*, there, in a shabby hotel at the end of the tramlines that ran out from Palma. Bob McAlmon, that strange American literary figure, was also living there, and we did a good deal of drinking together; he wrote of Majorca—and of me—in his autobiography, *Being Geniuses Together*,† but what he wrote about Majorca is more accurate than what he wrote about the development of our friendship; he wrote of 'the bums, cadgers, pretenders, and hangers-on of foreign colonies who quickly collect whenever a new place is located which is inexpensive, beautiful, and accessible'. What then were we ourselves

* Later Lieut-General Sir Frederick Browning, G.C.V.O., K.B.E., C.B., D.S.O. He died in 1965.
† 1938

doing there, it might be asked; the answer is simply that in the early Thirties, as in the Twenties, young writers and artists were still drifting about Europe, and for a time the Balearics were 'the place'; at least those lovely islands were not then 'tourist-ised' as now, and once you got away from Palma and the bars all was blessedly unspoiled.

All Experience was published in June, 1932, and I began drafting the novel Douglas Goldring had urged I should write, *Venetian Blinds*. He had insisted that the best part of the *Confessions* was the description of my childhood and youth in South London, and that I should put this material to further use, creatively, in fiction. It was sound advice and I acted on it. *Ragged Banners*, though written and published at the beginning of the Thirties, belonged in mood and manner to the Twenties; this 'proletarian's progress' was to be a kind of literary coming-of-age, and I think perhaps it was. It was the first sociological novel I had attempted, and I took a great deal of trouble over it.

In the early Thirties there was a spate of sociological novels. There were, outstandingly, A. J. Cronin's *Hatter's Castle*, in 1931, J. L. Hodson's *Harvest in the North*, in 1934, Walter Greenwood's *Love on the Dole*, in 1933, dramatised by Ronald Gow and produced on the London stage in 1934. There were the novels and short stories of James Hanley, who was, I suppose, *the* proletarian writer of the time. His novel, *Ebb and Flood*, about Liverpool dockers, published in 1932, was described as a novel of 'brutal realism', and a 'fine novel of working-class life'. Hanley himself was described as 'one of the really significant young writers of today'. In 1931 there had been his short stories, *Men in Darkness*, with a Preface by John Cowper Powys. They were described as 'terrible, powerful, remorseless'. Compton Mackenzie wrote of their 'quivering rawness', and Richard Aldington of the young writer's 'passion of pity and sensitive awareness of suffering'. John Cowper Powys declared that 'these striking and startling stories are very far removed from propaganda. They are much more terrible, much more shocking, much more moving than that. They are reality touched by the hand of art . . .'

Of the same *genre*, and winning similarly high praise, was F. C. Boden's novel, *Miner*, published in 1932. Boden was a miner and a poet; his verses attracted the attention of H. N Brailsford and later of Sir Arthur Quiller-Couch. His first book of poems, *Pit-head Poems*, was published in 1927, and a second book, *Out of the Coal-fields*, followed two years later. Thanks to the interest of various men of letters, notably Dr. Robert Bridges, the Poet Laureate, Boden was enabled to give up his work at the pit-head and study at University College, Exeter. *Miner* was acclaimed as the 'most important miners' book since Lawrence's *Sons and Lovers*. I thought very highly of this novel at the time, and looking at it again now, nearly forty years later, it still seems to me a very fine and powerful piece of work, and with more warmth to it than Hanley's 'brutal realism' . . . perhaps because Boden was a poet.

Such novels as *Miner, Ebb and Flood, Love on the Dole*—and there were many others—were labelled 'propaganda' novels, and in the sense that they were indictments of certain aspects of the social system, and campaigned, directly or implicitly, against such evils, they were, though I think that only *Love on the Dole* could be described as direct propaganda.

Walter Greenwood used to declare that I was his 'fairy godmother', because it was I who encouraged him to write the novel which made his name. He had sent me, out of the blue, some short stories—it is something which is liable to happen to authors, and usually the material sent is pretty poor and it is an embarrassment to make the requested comment on it; but this was material from someone who could obviously write. I replied suggesting it be used as a novel, for I couldn't see it finding a market as short stories. The author acted on my advice, and wrote it as the novel, *Love on the Dole*. We met and became friends, and when it was dramatised, with Wendy Hiller in the lead, I attended a rehearsal and met Ronald Gow—who later dramatised my mountaineering novel, *Men are Unwise*, but unfortunately without success; it was produced at a small theatre of the studio-club kind outside London and never reached the West End.

Walter Greenwood being in town for the rehearsals of *Love*

on the Dole I took him along to an I.L.P. dance, 'to meet some of the London revolutionary Left', and it was there that I met Reginald Reynolds, whom I was to marry three years later; I was introduced to him by Fenner Brockway, and danced with him, but I was light-headed with 'flu—I had only gone along because I had invited Walter Greenwood—and I left the dance early believing him to be Ronald Kidd of Civil Liberties, as I have recorded in *Privileged Spectator* . . . though why I didn't record how *Love on the Dole* came to be written I cannot imagine. I remember Walter Greenwood as a pleasant, sincere young man, quite unspoiled by success; we lost touch in later years; he returned to his native north, and there was the war, and anyhow life changes.

But what is important is that we who had been young in the Twenties were beginning with the onset of the Thirties to wave goodbye to the ideas and attitudes of that brash bright decade. The world was perceptibly changing; there was a sinister word which kept surfacing—*Fascism*. It wasn't new; it had been there in the Twenties with Mussolini, but it had not seemed so sinister and menacing then; we even made light of it—in Italy, we said, gaily, the trains run on time. But between 1930 and 1932 the National Socialists became the largest party in Germany, their emblem the crooked cross, and already those Jews who could do so were beginning to leave.

But for a while longer we went on going to Germany; until 1934, the year of what John Gunther, in *Inside Europe*,* called 'the trick by fire and the purge by blood', and the death of the old Wooden Titan, Hindenburg. It was the end of the sobering-up period; we were stone cold sober by then.

* 1936. Revised edition, 1938.

(*above*) Michael Arlen, whose romantic melodrama, *The Green Hat*, was a best-seller in 1924
(Radio Times Hulton Picture Library)

LITERARY CELEBRITIES
OF THE TWENTIES

(*right*) Radclyffe Hall (with Una, Lady Troubridge) whose novel, *The Well of Loneliness,* was prosecuted in 1928

The author, 1930. The 'jazz' background for this photograph was
specially designed by Ida Davies and was considered very modern
(Paul Tanqueray)

16

The wander years

In Germany in 1933 postcards of Hitler were on sale everywhere, and you could buy his effigy in chocolate; we were still
light-hearted enough about the funny little man with the Charlie Chaplin moustache to buy him in chocolate and think it
amusing to bite his head off, and to ask at newspaper kiosks and
bookstalls who was this Herr Hitler of whom there were so many
postcards, and to be told reverently that it was the Chancellor.
We ceased to be amused a little later when we found benches
in parks and streets labelled *Nicht für Juden. . . .*

Yet in retrospect those first three years of the Thirties do
seem a curious extension of the late Twenties, and up to 1933 I
think they were; the rise of the National Socialist Party in Germany did not seem particularly our business. Even as late as
1936 Lloyd George, who had accepted an invitation to Germany specially to meet Hitler, could declare of him, 'He is
indeed a great man. Führer is the proper name for him, for he
is a born leader. Yes, a statesman.' He added that one of the
things he liked about him was his 'directness of conversation . . .
He goes straight to the point without any subtle moves.' He
complimented Hitler, saying that he had accomplished a great
work, having restored Germany's honour.* Even later, in 1937,
Winston Churchill could write,† 'Those who have met Herr

---

* *The Real Lloyd George,* by A. J. Sylvester, 1947.
† *Great Contemporaries,* 1937 (page 268).

K

Hitler face to face in public business or on social terms have found a highly competent, cool, well-informed functionary with an agreeable manner, a disarming smile, and few have been un-affected by a subtle personal magnetism.' In the light of which —or the dark of which—that we who were young in the early Thirties and wandering round Europe were not seriously concerned would seem excusable.

I wrote most of *Commonsense and the Child* in the dark little hotel in the Rue des Beaux Arts, in the Latin Quarter of Paris, in the two-roomed 'suite' in which Oscar Wilde died, as I have told in *Privileged Spectator*. Most of *Linda Shawn*, *Venetian Blinds*, and a mountaineering novel entitled *Men are Unwise*, were written in Paris in a modern private hotel in a room looking into the chestnut trees of the Avenue de l'Ob-servatoire. It was whilst I was living in 'the Oscar Wilde hotel', as we always called it, and eating in a cheap little restaurant in the Rue St. Benoît, in the Quarter, that I saw Stanislas Idzikov-ski, who was with the Diaghileff Ballet until 1926, and who had been so memorable as the Bluebird in *Aurora's Wedding*. He rejoined Diaghileff in 1928 and I must have seen him in many other ballets, but it is his Bluebird I have always remembered.

The 'Oscar Wilde hotel' has recently been acquired by young men of 'progressive' ideas, who have refurbished it and made a patio of the little neglected walled garden with the fig tree into which I looked as I sat writing *Commonsense and the Child*, and the short stories I collected into a volume I called *Dryad*, most of which had a Paris setting. This was my second collection of short stories, the first, *Green Figs*, having been published late in 1931; these are mostly child stories, but a long story, *Surbiton to Montparnasse*, was originally planned as a chapter for *Pil-grims*, but was cut because the novel was too long. The first story in the book, *Apple-Christening*, was the nucleus of *Linda Shawn*.

There were a number of American writers around in Paris in those years, notably Kay Boyle and her husband, Laurence Vail, who were later in Vienna, with John Gunther and his wife. Gunther had not then written *Inside Europe*, the first of his 'Inside' books, but had a reputation as a live newspaper man, and he was a very pleasant, easy, likable personality who was always good company. I drafted the mountaineering novel, *Men are Unwise*, in Hamburg in the spring of 1933 and finished it in Vienna in the winter. There were many homosexuals, of both sexes, in Vienna at that time, because Hitler had been cleaning up the homosexual *boîtes* in Berlin and Hamburg, which until then had been 'gay' in all senses. I recorded in *Privileged Spectator*: 'Vienna was full of parasites, mostly foreign, and full, too, of destitute people, whole families in the gutter, and queues of down-and-outs lining up outside the big cafés and restaurants for scraps.' The 'parasites' were *rentiers*—there seemed to be a great many of them in the Twenties and early Thirties, anyhow in the literary and artistic circles—who were 'refugees', as it were, from what we derisively referred to as 'expurgated Berlin'. Vienna, not yet expurgated, obliged with a number of homosexual dancing places and bars. In the hangover from the Twenties this sort of thing was still considered 'amusing'. But in literary huddles round the tall tiled stoves, in the apartments we rented from the impoverished Viennese, the talk was more of Jean Cocteau and Gertrude Stein than of the Führer who was cleaning up Berlin.

It was all completely crazy. We all had perfectly good homes, but there we were renting shabby Viennese apartments, checking into dark *Kaiserliche* little hotels, or, in Paris, in dark Left Bank hotels with frightful wallpaper and abominable plumbing. Why did we do it? The answer is simple: running round Europe was the vogue with the young intelligentsia of the period, both English and American. We worked, of course; I recall a party of eight of us driving out into the Viennese countryside and no less than five of us being 'with book'.

In Paris I frequented the bars and cafés and night places in Montparnasse and in the Champs-Elyées collecting bright social chit-chat for *The Bystander* letter. When that finished I went South. The Vails took a villa above Villefranche, and I—staying at the Welcome Hotel, fashionable with the intelligentsia because Cocteau had stayed there—visited them there and met 'Sacha' Berkman, the Russian anarchist. Berkman, it will be recalled, had served thirteen years of a twenty-two-year sentence in America for his attempted assassination of Henry Clay Frick, Chairman of the Carnegie Steel Company, during an industrial dispute. At that time Berkman had been the lover of Emma Goldman, another Russian Jewish anarchist, and in 1932 he was living at her villa in St. Tropez with her, and his post-prison mistress, 'Emmy'—an unhappy *ménage à trois* of which Emma, with her fund-raising efforts for the martyr-hero, Alexander Berkman, was the main support. Four years later Berkman killed himself in Nice, on Emma's birthday, shooting himself in the stomach, the frightful strain of this complicated relationship having proved too much. I did not meet Emma in the South of France, though she was a friend of the Vails; she was not at the party at which I met Berkman—and danced with him and longed to talk with him, but was somehow constrained by his own reserve; I met her in London the following year, and the meeting was somewhat negative. But when she went back to St. Tropez we corresponded; she read some of my books and became interested, and when she came to London during the Spanish Civil War I worked with her, in support of the struggle of the Spanish anarchists, speaking with her at public meetings, raising money for 'arms for Spain'. After the defeat we campaigned for the refugees. She was a remarkable and immensely courageous but extremely difficult woman, her personality repellent—domineering, aggressive, both in her public and private relationships. After her death in Canada—she was not allowed to return to U.S.A.—in 1940, I told her story in a novel I called *Red Rose**—she was always known as 'Red Emma'. She had often urged that when they were all dead she and Berkman and 'Emmy' I should write their story.

By the time I met 'Red Emma, Queen of the Anarchists', in London again I had been twice to Russia; in 1934, briefly, going only to Moscow for the Theatre Festival, and in 1935, extensively, making the then forbidden journey, illegally, to Samarkand, and returning *persona non grata* with the authorities, and as disillusioned as Emma herself had been in the exciting early days of the Revolution.

But the 1934 visit, although it produced a certain amount

* 1941.

of misgiving, was nevertheless 'all a wonder and a wild desire'
—to believe. At that time we of the Left did very much want to
believe in the glorious Workers' Republic, suppressing doubts
and criticisms, at least in print, for fear, as we put it, of 'playing
into the hands of reactionaries'. It was a long way from the
Twenties by then, but we were still nothing if not progressive,
and politically conscious as never before.

17

Comrade, O Comrade!

This is the title of an ironic little book I subtitled, 'A Low-Down on the Left', published in 1946, and which was really an expression of my scepticism concerning all the Left parties and groups—Communists, Trotskyists, Labourites, Anarchists, the lot. But when I wrote the Socialist Summer School chapter in *Forever Wandering*, in 1934, I believed in it all, took it all very seriously—'here were no "intellectual socialists",' I wrote, 'but real workers for a cause in which they believed not merely intellectually but with a profound personal passion. It is this sacred fire which is rebuilding Russia.'

When I attended that Independent Labour Party Summer School, in the summer of 1934, I had not been to Russia, but just before I had met a friend, Hubert Griffiths, at the Ballet. He was planning to leave with a small party for Moscow for the Theatre Festival, and he did so with the object of collecting material for a book on 'Russia at Play', which would consist of essays by various people, with himself as editor; he suggested that I should join the party and collect material for a chapter for the book on the Children's Theatre. He and his party were travelling by Soviet ship to Leningrad, and on to Moscow by train. The idea appealed to me very strongly, for it was inevitable that, *enfant du siècle* as I still was, I should eventually visit Russia, and this seemed an opportunity; but I was not free—for various domestic reasons—to leave at that time. It was suggested that I could perhaps fly out later; I said that I would think about it whilst at the Summer School and give him my reply on my return. I kept my promise most meticulously by lunching with him on the very day I got back from Newport, Monmouthshire, where the Summer School was held. I went straight from the station to his club, still clutching the bunch of pink roses bought for me in Newport market by an Indian comrade. The Summer School, it seems, had tipped the scales in favour of my going to Russia. I recorded:* 'We talked practical details for a little while, and then when all was settled, he asked, "And did you have a good time at the Summer School?"

'I told him with truth, "I've not enjoyed myself so much since I was in America."

' "Wasn't it," he asked, "all rather art-and-crafty—lemonade and Lenin, Marxism and milk?"

' "We did," I said, "drink lemonade, and milk, and we did talk of Marxism, and the name of Lenin was mentioned. And Gandhi. And we played Nuts-in-May."

' "No," he protested. "Not Nuts-in-May. 'We'll have Jimmy Maxton to fetch her away.' I can't bear it!"

' "You'll have to," I said. "I liked it."

' "My God, Socialists at play! Who was it said it isn't the isms it's the ists? Have some more sherry—you must be needing it after all that lemonade and nut-and-maying."

' "There was," I told him, "a tavern in the town . . ." and suddenly was heartsick for those eager faces, people I knew only by their Christian names [were there no Jews amongst them, I now ask myself] and might never see again. Comrades! I found myself thinking there was no finer word in the language.

'I fingered the drooping roses.

' "Tell me more about Russia," I said.'

I find this, now, a very period piece of writing. It seems one really did care about that abstraction called the Revolution, and that materialisation of the revolutionary dream called the U.S.S.R. Of the audience for a Maxton lecture at the Summer School I wrote: 'Crowded into the lecture hall of that gaunt grey training college perched up on the Welsh hills that summer

* *Forever Wandering*, 1934.

morning were men and women of all ages, all trades and professions, grey-haired husbands and wives seated side by side, boys and girls in shorts—youth predominating—men and women of one faith, gathered together under one flag. . . .They who would build a new world must first overthrow the old; they must revolutionise, not compromise; re-create out of the fire of their dreams, not temporise with the collapsing and outworn. This they know who were assembled in that lecture-hall that morning, faces intent, eyes upon their leader, their spirit answering his. Out of this knowledge springs their enthusiasm, their courage, their unquenchable hope.'

There is more, much more, in a similar exalted strain. Did I not say that it was relatively an Age of Innocence? Such innocent pranks we got up to, when we were not kindling the pure flame of revolutionary fervour : Jimmy Maxton with a coloured handkerchief tied round his head singing 'The Pirate King', and at the fancy-dress ball a fair-haired young man going as Ethel Mannin, in my clothes, lending me his grey flannels and red shirt meantime, and, of course, another young man pulling a lock of hair over his forehead and going as Hitler, and strolling arm in arm with Dollfuss, and Fenner Brockway in arrow-sewn pyjamas as Public Enemy Number Three, and, inevitably, a Russian peasant.

And on the last day, in the small hours of the morning, no less inevitably, 'Auld Lang Syne' and then the Internationale.

Comrades, O Comrades!

How could I not accept the invitation to Moscow after that?

London–Moscow by air was quite a business in 1934. The four o'clock in the afternoon 'plane—very small and hot, and with only eight other passengers—to Berlin, a night in Berlin, then at seven in the morning a 'plane for Danzig and Königsberg, 'where one transfers from the German machine to a German-Russian one'. Danzig is reached at nine, and in less than an hour Königsberg, and the frontier is crossed at Wladiszlawow, and shortly after this we descend at Kaunas, the capital of Lithuania. It is by then midday. We descend on Russian soil at five in the afternoon—seven Russian time, and I exult, 'At last I am in Russia !' But it is another two and a half hours on to Moscow. A large framed portrait of Lenin stares down on the Customs proceedings . . . which take an hour, but at last I am 'whirled away in a car along a tree-lined boulevard flanked by tall modern blocks of flats and through streets bright with lighted shops. Dim blue domes powdered with golden stars flashed past. There was a smell on the air that reminded me of Paris. Moscow! I wanted to laugh aloud with pure joy.' I am asked if I feel up to going to the theatre that night, a seat has been reserved for me—*La Dame aux Camélias*; it began half an hour ago but would be going on for hours yet—'all Russian theatres begin at half past seven and go on till midnight'. Despite a raging headache after the twelve-hour flight in the small hot 'plane I agree to go, but first I am taken to the big Metropole Hotel, before the Revolution the de luxe hotel of the city, and still with a faded splendour of plush and chandeliers. I am fed with caviar and chicken, cream cakes and wine, in the vast dining-room with a fountain the middle and a deafeningly loud orchestra on a dais. Then to the theatre, where 'in suffocating heat the lady of the camellias dies her wearisome death'. The play was received with wild applause at the end of each act, 'and nobody seemed to find the chronic over-acting in the least comic'. But a production of *The Cherry Orchard* 'seemed to me in every way superior to that of either the Little Theatre or Old Vic productions in London, and it was played with a brisker sense of comedy'. But the Ballet I found 'less good than the de Basil company, and the production disappointingly old-fashioned, in the manner of a provincial pantomime'. But I was in Moscow primarily to see the children's theatres, of which there were four, and these I found admirable—except for the crude propaganda of an anti-fascist play—and I was very much impressed. I wrote at length about the Children's Theatre in the book edited by Hubert Griffiths, *Playtime in Russia*, published in 1935. 'The sets and the music are in the best modern tradition,' I wrote, 'and the whole cannot have other than an immense cultural value for the child. I liked very much, too, the atmosphere of the theatre, the feeling that here was not merely a theatre attended mainly by children, but a real children's club where they could feel free and at ease.' But a state nursery at which mothers left their children whilst at work I found a depressing place, unhygienic and unimaginative, the children listless and pale, and some with the appearance of being positively unhappy. I wrote about this also in *Forever Wandering*, equally frankly, though in general I was anxious to leave with the reader a good impression of the Soviet Union. I declared that in Russia 'progress was a reality, not a newspaper catch-phrase, a life illuminated by an ideal—the ideal of the right to live, as opposed to merely existing, for every man'. Did I really believe that? Certainly I didn't after the 1935 visit, which was extensive and unconducted; but in 1934? There were things other than the nursery I hadn't liked, and some of it I recorded, but with the defence that Russia was still in a state of transition, that it was the country of the future. It was a case, I think, not only for me but for a number of us who visited Russia at that time, of 'Lord, I believe; help thou my unbelief'.

It is interesting that for this Griffiths book Marie Rambert and Lesley Blanch reported on 'Some Impressions of the Ballet in Russia in 1934', and that they wrote: 'Here in the original home of the ballet it is still the dancing of the individual rather than the production as a whole which counts; in fact from the point of view of technique the ballet is just as good—and just as bad—as before the Revolution.' They found that two political—'propaganda'—ballets rather palled on the audience, and despite the new and revolutionary themes were danced 'in the dead idiom of an old-fashioned opera'. For the dancing in *Swan Lake* they had the highest praise, but not for the *mise en scène*, with rainbow lights and a real fountain playing, of which they said Oh dear! They conclude their piece, however, with no misgivings as to the future of Soviet ballet. It was to be another twenty-seven years before Nureyev, in an assertion of his individualism, the artist's right to be free, defected to the West.

It was in the Metropole Hotel, during that first visit to Russia in the autumn of 1934, that I met Ernst Toller, though for some reason I do not mention this in the 'Moscow Notes' in *Forever Wandering*, or any of the people I met except Maurice Hindus. But I wrote about it in *Privileged Spectator*, and how we 'walked together in the moonlight under the white walls of the Kremlin and in the shadows of the fantastic domes and spires of St. Basil's, and laughed and were gay because it was Moscow and the stars were bright and thick as a field of daisies and the air as electric as spring'. I had very much wanted to meet Ernst Toller after reading his moving autobiography, *I was a German* (the original title was *Eine Jugend in Deutschland*) translated by Edward Crankshaw and published in England early in 1934. In an introduction to it, written on the day his books were burnt in Germany, Toller wrote: 'Not only my own youth is portrayed here, but also the youth of a whole generation, and a slice of history into the bargain.' As a Jew and a revolutionary there was no place for Toller in Nazi Germany. He was a man of immense personal charm and revolutionary courage, and I admired him immensely, even when I did not always agree with him, and I loved him dearly. That he should finally, in America, in May, 1939, take his own life was most tragic and terrible, and a fearful shock to many of us. The *Birmingham Mail*, May 23, 1939, reporting his death wrote: 'It is a strange coincidence that this tragedy should have followed so soon after the publication of Ethel Mannin's new book (*Privileged Spectator*), in which is described how she and Toller vainly endeavoured to persuade the late W. B. Yeats to intervene on behalf of that other notable victim of the Nazi regime, Ossietzky, who at that time was languishing in a German prison.'

The friendship begun in Moscow was maintained in London, and we met for the last time, by chance, in a street during the Munich crisis; if the war came, he declared, we must fight; war would not destroy Fascism, I said, only human lives. The deep disagreement was terrible to us both. We embraced and parted and did not meet again, and a few months later came the shattering news of his tragic end. There were so many of us who would have helped him, if only we had known.

I met Donia Nachshen in Moscow at that time. She was standing on the steps of the Metropole Hotel; she was not staying in that hotel and I had not known she was in Moscow. I had met her in London; Norman Haire had brought her out to the cottage to lunch. Nothing had come of that meeting, but in Moscow we developed a friendship. She was Russian-Jewish and ardently pro-Russia. 'We neither of us dreamed we should be back in Moscow together the following year,' I wrote, 'committed to the forbidden journey to Samarkand.' I left Moscow in 1934 convinced that I should return to it; I did not then contemplate going as far afield as Turkestan; this idea grew out of a friendship with another of the proletarian writers of the time, James Whittaker. Like Greenwood, he had come to London from the north; he had published his autobiography, *I, James Whittaker,** which I had reviewed and praised, and we got in touch. He was working for a publishing house and keen to get books for them; he suggested that I should go to Russia again and write a book about it this time—for his firm. This time, too, I should go further afield; make a really big thing of it. We pored over maps together and there grew up in us the idea of the Forbidden Journey, the Golden Journey, to Samarkand. Nowadays, of course, anyone who has the time and the money can get there through one of those package holiday schemes; but not in 1935; you needed a permit, then, for Turkestan, and the U.S.S.R. was almost never issuing permits for Turkestan; the odd traveller was getting there illegally—Ella Maillart, the Swiss traveller, whom I got to know, was one; she wrote a book about her adventure, *Turkestan Solo*, published in 1934. There had been some organised tours to Samarkand before 1935, under the auspices of the Russian travel organisation, Intourist; the tourists lived on the train and were taken on conducted sightseeing trips, but such tours were not available when I conceived the idea of going to Turkestan, and I should not have wanted to go there in that way even if there had been. The story of that illegal journey is told in the book I wrote on my return, *South to Samarkand*, published in 1936, though not by the publishers for whom James Whittaker worked, for I was under contract to give my regular publishers the first offer of everything I wrote, and they wanted this book. I made the journey with Donia Nachshen, who was to have illustrated the

* 1934.

book, but who, when she read what I had written, withdrew from the arrangement, feeling unable to co-operate in a book she considered 'anti-Soviet' . . . which it was; or anyhow unsympathetic. The book was the story of a disillusionment.

Before I could set out on 'the golden road to Samarkand' I had to finish the novel I was working on, *The Pure Flame*, a sequel to *Cactus*, which had been published early that year and which I had dedicated to Ernst Toller; it foretold the Spanish Civil War: '. . . there was Russia in 1917, Germany in 1919, England in 1926, Austria in this year of revolt, 1934. And the end is not yet. Soon out of the rich warm soil of Spain will come revolt, from the Basque country and Catalonia . . . and possibly as in America, as in Austria, the workers will go down for the count, and the troops fire on the people, one mass of workers in uniform against another mass in uniform and without. But soldiers and workers have been in council for their common good before, and will be again, for that is the history of mankind, which is the history of revolt.'

The Pure Flame, which was a novel of working-class life, was dedicated to James Whittaker, as an appreciation of his own courageous proletarian struggle, not only against dire poverty but ill-health. The novel preached the Revolution, and according to the publishers' blurb on the dust-cover, 'ends on a note of hope, with youth pledging itself to the expiation of the injustices and inequalities of the past, and listening to the footsteps of a great and growing army marching under a red banner, the footsteps of happiness drawing nearer'. The blurb concludes with the belief that 'this novel will give the author of *Venetian Blinds* and of *Cactus* a place amongst contemporary women novelists which in the masculine field is occupied by such writers as Dr. Cronin and J. L. Hodson'. The hope was unfulfilled; I did not continue in this strain; disillusionment with the U.S.S.R. somewhat quenched the pure flame of revolutionary ardour.

I completed the revision of *The Pure Flame* in the Soviet ship to Leningrad. James Whittaker had had for a time the crazy notion of joining Donia and me on the trip—crazy because his health would never have stood up to so arduous a journey, and one which, as it turned out, was to prove a great deal more arduous than we had bargained for, because of our illegal status once we had crossed the Caspian—but was forced to abandon it.

We left in October, the month in which Mussolini invaded Abyssinia; it seemed madness to be leaving home when anything might happen and people were asking themselves anxiously whether if 'sanctions' were applied to Italy it might lead to World War II; but we felt ourselves committed to the adventure, and in 1935 it was still possible to believe that the worst would not happen. In my own case there was a double conflict about leaving, for in July I had met Reginald Reynolds again and I was seriously in love.

But Donia and I set out, and the story of this far from golden journey is told in the book I subsequently wrote, *South to Samarkand*, published after *The Pure Flame* the following year. It is a story of frustration—we spent ten days in Moscow trying to get permits for Turkestan and finally left without them— and such physical hardships as travelling fourth class across the Caspian, which meant dossing down on the deck, and sleeping on Samarkand railway station because without proper 'papers', which we lacked, you cannot get a bed, even in a lodging-house, in Turkestan, and making the return journey 'hard', which is very hard indeed—as hard as the 'soft' by which we had travelled as far as the Caspian, as guests of the Soviet government, is luxuriously soft. But I had achieved my objective and reached the then forbidden Samarkand, but whereas when I got back from the U.S.S.R. in 1934 I had dreamed of returning, I returned from the 1935 journey quothing the raven, and the last word in the book in which I recorded the journey is *Nevermore*.

18

The Jubilee Year

The late Charles Duff wrote in his book, *England and the English*, published in 1954: 'In the 1930's there was not only the general feeling of economic crisis—a feeling impossible to avoid, what with all kinds of stringencies and a vast and growing mass of unemployment—but once again came a touch of the feeling which some had felt in the pre-1914 period. . . . Perhaps for the first time in a century and a half England felt *unsure* of herself, worried and suffering from a lack of clear and vigorous leadership.' England had been affected by the Wall Street slump, and tackled the financial crisis by forming, in August, 1931, a National Government of all three parties, designed to balance the Budget and save the pound. Nevertheless in September England came off the gold standard, and, in banking language, 'the pound sterling dropped to 80 per cent of its par value', and the country was cast into gloom. The government, 'by a series of Draconic measures which struck at everybody', says Charles Duff, 'avoided recourse to borrowing; and the pound recovered to steady itself, though well below parity. The powerful national Press, and the news broadcast on the radio, added to the gloom. There could be no disguising the fact that England was again living in a time of crisis.'

R. H. Mottram, in his book, *The Twentieth Century, a Personal Record*,* after noting 'unemployment, financial unsound-

* 1969.

ness and political mistrust', and the announcement of a
'National Government'—the inverted commas are his—upon
which he made a note in his diary, he tells us, 'Whatever that is,'
goes on to say that 'the features of the 1930's which made most
impression was the possibility not so much of a change of government as of a change of the entire political scheme into something much more akin to one or all of the various dictatorships
that nearly all the European countries had had (literally) forced
upon them. In Great Britain this tendency or movement was
given the name of 'Blackshirts'. Its leader, Sir Oswald Mosley,
saw rightly that he had a very good opportunity to bring about
such a change. He speaks of the then 'hardly healed financial
stress', and the 'obvious confusion in the Liberal and Labour
parties', which made 'any kind of government by majority rule
look suspect'. It seemed to him that the 'Blackshirt disciplined
membership looked in many ways better than anything we
seemed likely to get at the moment, certainly better than Communist dictatorship appeared to produce'. He considered that
neither Baldwin nor MacDonald were capable of leading the
country, and that 'everything played into Mosley's hands, in
this island and throughout the articulate world'. That there
were a great many people who believed that Mosley's British
Union of Fascists presented an alternative to what was for them
the greater evil of Communism, and might prove an effective
force, is undoubtedly true. With his strong-hand-in-India line
he won approval from the die-hard imperialists and the upper
middle classes, and he declared, confidently, 'If a mandate be
conferred on us by the people at a General election, then this is a
dictatorship by the will of the people, expressing for themselves
what they want.' My own view-from-the-bridge, the view of
the young Left intelligentsia, was quite different. To us it looked
ugly; there were numerous incidents of young black-shirted
thugs acting aggressively and provocatively towards Communists and working-class East End Jews. Mosley's 'disciplined' fol-
lowers angered and disgusted us, but we did not take the movement seriously as a potential political power.

But in spite of the feeling that 'it couldn't happen here',
meaning the horror of Fascism, 1934 was a politically anxious

year, with the civil war in Austria, and Italian troops mustering
at the frontier after the murder of Dollfuss, and people nervously reminding each other that the 1914 War had started
with an assassination in Central Europe. Fear and anxiety really
began in that year, but neither what Mottram, and a good many
people like him, he says, 'grudgingly' prepared themselves for,
nor what I, and a good many people like me, dreaded, happened
that year; there were, in fact, still five years to, and in the spring
of 1935 the country moved into a curious national euphoria
produced by the Silver Jubilee of King George and Queen
Mary. Mottram says that 'in its broadest, historical sense, what
happened was a resurgence of the English capacity for keeping
politics in their place'.

John Gunther* puts it rather differently : 'The Jubilee, silver
in name, was worth its weight in gold. Not only did it symbolise
the return of comparative prosperity to Britain (and incidentally
bring millions of pounds in trade to London), but it expressed
with great brilliance the affection with which the nation regarded the Royal Family. The King was intensely touched,
and, since he was a modest man, astounded at the colossal mass
emotion his presence evoked. The origins of the Jubilee were
obscure. There was no precedent for the celebration of the
twenty-fifth anniversary of the accession of a monarch. No one,
when the matter was first discussed in the House of Commons,
anticipated the depth and range of celebration that occurred.'

The *Daily Mail* declared it 'England's happiest week since
the war ended'. The week began on May 6—a perfect, golden
day, 'King's weather', the Press called it, and it was a week of
carnival, of dancing in the streets, and extended licensing laws.
There were flags everywhere, and the meaner the streets the
thicker the flags. In the slums there were banners, 'Lousy, but
loyal'. Street tea parties were organised for the children. The
golden weather held, and the week was one long bank holiday.
The Press was jubilant; everyone was jubilant, even the *Daily
Herald*, which, I recorded bitterly, was more royalist than the
King. 'Given enough press propaganda,' I wrote, in 1938, 'you
can get the British masses to turn out for anything in the nature

* In *Inside Europe.*

L

of a "show"; and the English dearly love a pageant and an ex-
cuse for a bank-holiday atmosphere.' True enough, but why
so bitter? I now ask myself. It wasn't for me then, and it
wouldn't be for me now, but *chacun à son goût*. I have never
liked crowds or been able to feel myself part of any particular
occasion; as I see it, this doesn't make me any better or worse
than those who dearly love a tamasha; it is simply the way I am.
But young in the Twenties I was still young enough in the early
Thirties to be impatient—'O Lord, what *fools* these mortals be !'
—and intolerant. The perfervid patriotism was undoubtedly
whipped up by the Press, and I doubt if there could be quite
such an uprush of inspired emotionalism nowadays, what with
television sophistication, and the stock of royalty being a long
way short of what it was then. A friend of mine who was a
young newspaper man at the time, and with whom I discussed
the year 1935, wrote me : 'You will remember the madness of
the Silver Jubilee when King George on his tours discovered to
his amazement that he was popular.'

My objection to monarchy—to any monarchy—is not merely
that in this day and age it is an anachronism, but that it rests on
a basis of false values—the adulation of very ordinary people
who but for their exalted position would pass unremarked, lacking any particular intellectual distinction or artistic accomplish-
ment, or, for the most part, anything special in the way of looks,
qualities of character, or charisma. They are also absurdly expensive. A president would be a very great deal cheaper, even
commanding a very high salary. For one thing we should not be
called upon to subsidise his family and in-laws.

But in the Jubilee year of 1935 royalty's stock was high, and
their uninteresting lives were considered highly newsworthy.
In January, 1935, the Press splashed the story of the Duchess of
Kent's first trip in an aeroplane. ('I enjoyed it very much,' she
said.) In July the Press had a royal 'real love match' to be sloppy
about—the engagement of the Duke of Gloucester to Alice
Montagu-Douglas-Scott, daughter of the Duke and Duchess of
Buccleuch and Queensberry. This overflowed into the following
summer, when the Lady Alice visited Balmoral and curtsied to
the Queen who stood on the steps to receive her, and 'a crowd

of fifty tenants and servants and their wives who had been given special permission to be present watched the little scene'.

The Jubilee slopped over, too, beyond the golden week in May, and when an ape was born in the London Zoo it was named Jubilee; so was a new chocolate bar.

Sir Stafford Cripps, however, was in trouble for running down the Jubilee and declaring it was made the occasion for 'political ballyhoo'. The First Commissioner of Works, Mr. Ormsby-Gore, said it made him sick 'for a man like Sir Stafford to go up and down the country organising class hatred'.

In the early spring, we had had Epstein's second sculpture of Christ, 'Behold the Man!', about which there was as much fuss as over his 'Rima' in 1929. By that time some of us who had been young in the Twenties no longer felt it necessary to lean over backwards to admire whatever was 'modern'; I was thirty-four by that time and did not mind saying out loud that I thought this grotesque seated figure of Christ quite horrible. The *Daily Mirror* refused to publish a photograph of it, and G. K. Chesterton applauded their action; he regarded the statue, he said, as one of the greatest insults to religion he had ever seen. He called the work an 'outrage', as did the novelist, Mary Borden; she felt that Epstein knew nothing about the man he had called Christ. The *Catholic Times* called the statue 'an Asiatic monstrosity', declared it 'an insult offered to Christ', and 'ugly and vile'. As against this, T. W. ('Tommy') Earp defended the work in a long critique in the *Daily Telegraph*, declaring that 'it has the authority of tradition behind it', and referring to the 'impressive energy' of its 'self-contained rhythm' —whatever that may mean. James Bone also defended the work in the *Manchester Guardian*, calling it a 'caratyd of suffering', and referring to the 'sense of crushing agony bearing upon the squat enduring figure crowned with thorns'. Anthony Blunt in the *Spectator* declared it 'unquestionably a work of religious art', whilst acknowledging that it 'represents an approach to the problem new at any rate in England'. Epstein, he said, had 'vivified European religious art by an infusion of dark blood, itself not pure but drawn from the African, the Aztec and many other races'. Epstein himself said of the work, in his autobiography, *Let There be Sculpture*, published in 1940, that he wished to make an Ecce Homo, 'a symbol of man, bound, crowned with thorns and facing with as relentless and over-mastering gaze of pity and prescience our unhappy world'.

The sculpture was shown in the Leicester Galleries, then in Leicester Square, with other works—portrait heads and busts—and the gallery was, of course, far too small for the display of so massive a work. Anthony Blunt said that it should be placed in a church, 'where it would be seen from a distance and make its appeal instantly'.

Epstein was always astonished by the intensity of the attacks on his works; he could accept it from art critics, but the 'almost insane hatred of the average man and woman' he found baffling. He failed to understand that it was the average man and woman who were baffled; that there was no hatred, only a sense of outrage; simply, Jesus was not like that; even as a 'symbol of man' he was not like that, heavy, brutish, grotesque—a monster.

Other things happened that March besides the Epstein exhibition: Germany ordered conscription, and the British Cabinet was called on a Sunday to discuss it; Mussolini called up more troops, declaring that he would 'back peace with millions of bayonets'; the great liner, the *Mauretania*, known as the 'gayest ship afloat', was retired. At the end of April there was the news that Germany was building submarines again, but we were going to have a Silver Jubilee on May 6, and were busy organising local fêtes and putting out more flags.

I spent some time in a convent that summer in order to finish *The Pure Flame*. The diary notes made at the time read like history-and-old-times. A friend drove me to the convent and we 'dined at Croydon aerodrome' *en route* and sat on a terrace and 'looked out over a little garden to the flying field. . . .'

On returning from the convent I continued to work on the novel, and according to the diary 'went a good deal to the Ballet'. I recorded that for me it was 'an interesting, happy summer, that Jubilee summer of 1935, and leading all the time to the golden road to Samarkand'. They were days, it seemed, 'of ballets, and dreams of Samarkand, and happiness'. In the

Twenties there was gaiety, and the word 'amusing' came into it a good deal, but in the much less gay Thirties, it seems, there was something called happiness; a curiously dated word it seems now, and by the end of the decade already less serviceable.

Nineteen-thirty-four had been the year of fear and anxiety, though at home we had had the wedding of the beautiful and fashionable Princess Marina—something new then in royalty —to the Duke of Kent, 'amid national rejoicing'. But 1935 was the Jubilee year, and the euphoria of that week in May lasted down through the lovely summer; there had not yet been the rape of Ethiopia, and pacifism was all the rage. It really did seem like that—a craze, with a nation-wide Peace Ballot and the founding of the Peace Pledge Union in June. The previous autumn there had been a great sending of postcards to Canon Dick Sheppard of St. Martin-in-the-Fields, saying that the senders renounced war, would never support or sanction another, and would do all in their power to persuade others to act likewise. I did not myself send a postcard or join the P.P.U., but all through 1935 I was strongly pacifist, and under Reginald's Gandhian influence became not merely anti-war but dedicated to the idea of non-violence generally. I am not being cynical when I say that in 1934 and 1935 pacifism was 'fashionable', especially among the young intelligentsia, along with what in the I.L.P. we called 'critical support of the Soviet Union'. As Ronald Blythe says in *The Age of Illusion,** writing of the Thirties, 'By mid-decade art talk and sex talk were out and political talk was in. It absorbed every stratum of society and the mass entertainers were obliged to note the trend and cater for it.'

Reginald was secretary of the No More War Movement in those years, and the National Council for Civil Liberties came into being, with E. M. Forster as its President. In February, 1933, Dr. C. E. M. Joad spoke at the Oxford Union on the motion 'that this House will in no circumstance fight for its king and country', and carried the motion by 275 votes to 152. As Reginald commented in his autobiography this triumph for pacifism 'certainly shook a good many people and appeared to put pacifists on the map as people to be taken seriously'.

* 1963.

Such distinguished personalities as Aldous Huxley and Gerald Heard—whose new book, *The Source of Civilisation*, appeared in 1935—were associated with the fashionable trend. Reginald reviewed Heard's book enthusiastically and it led to a correspondence. Heard wanted Reginald to tell him about Gandhi, non-violence, and Gandhi's American disciple, Richard Gregg, and proposed a meal at his flat. I have forgotten now where the flat was, but it was somewhere in the West End of London and a rather grand address, and very clearly I recollect wondering whether Reginald, as much a Quaker in the simplicity of his tastes as in his religious convictions, essentially *Gandhian*, would feel at home, but he was very keen to meet Heard and tell him about Gandhi, from his first-hand knowledge of him, and he went along. As it turned out he did not tell Heard anything at all, for Heard did all the talking; it was brilliant, but it was a monologue. Reginald was nevertheless very interested, for Heard outlined a plan in which he said Huxley was also interested : groups of like-minded people were to be formed for 'self-training' in putting the pacifist line across; they were to equip themselves for a kind of spiritual crusade. To me it sounded intolerably high falutin', but Reginald found it exciting that Huxley was interested, and at the next meeting with Heard he also met Huxley, but, he recorded,* 'Huxley proved a disappointment. I had hoped to find him as communicative as his books, and as witty. Instead I had met a taciturn character who talked in brief sentences, not always audibly, peering at one from behind his thick lenses in a way which made one uncomfortably aware of being scrutinised by the inscrutable. His very silence made one chatter nervously and foolishly, cursing oneself all the time for each word spoken. I felt that I knew Huxley much better from a brief correspondence with him, twelve years later, than I did from meeting him several times in 1935.'

The self-training group was formed and Reginald attended several meetings, but, as I had anticipated, never felt at home in it—he was too essentially down-to-earth. In his own words, 'By 1935 I was becoming a little sceptical of purely political action, but I was still too intent on quick results to be patient with a

* In *My Life and Crimes*.

group which practised silent meditation.' He wrote to Heard that he felt a misfit and Heard replied kindly, 'Probably you are right but in a way I'm sorry. It was perhaps early to be sure of doubts as to value. What is more important, though, is to ask you, if you find what you are looking for, to let us know.' Reginald liked that; it was, he declared, a reply worthy of Gandhi himself.

At that time, mid-decade, apart from membership of the Independent Labour Party, Reginald and I were active in various freedom groups and committees, notably in the African Freedom Campaign, and the Indian Freedom Campaign—though with his Indian experience Reginald was more active than I was in the latter. Being 'active' meant speaking at public meetings, writing articles, raising funds, distributing literature—in a word *campaigning*. There was also the Irish Anti-Partition campaign, but I did not become associated with this until later in the Thirties. Mid-Thirties anti-fascism became as fashionable as pacifism and various anti-fascist committees were set up. Reginald and I were as deeply opposed to Fascism as we were to Stalinism, and for the same reason, an endemic fear and hatred of totalitarianism in any form, but we were not active on the anti-fascist front until 1936 and the Spanish Civil War. In 1935 we were more concerned with opposing Imperialism; there were plenty of people—outstandingly the Communists —opposing Fascism, which at that time did not demand to be taken as seriously as the urgent problems of anti-imperialism.

'The Fascists', Reginald wrote, 'had set a new political fashion, which their enemies were not slow to imitate, of baiting and threatening their opponents and, where possible, breaking up their meetings. The old liberal tradition of free speech was probably never more in danger, in this country, than it was in that decade.' The spirit of the Thirties was particularly evoked for him by an advertisement in an evening newspaper, advertising the 'Moseley Rubber Truncheon'. Price six shillings. Post free from an address in Manchester. Its virtue—that it 'lays a man out without mess'. It had, of course, nothing to do with the Fascist leader, the spelling of the name was different, and it

was made by a firm that manufactured tyres, but Reginald cherished the cutting he clipped from the newspaper for years, because, he suspected, his 'inflamed imagination saw in it some
evil machination of the British Union of Fascists'.

In 1935 the Blackshirts were our political enemies, like the
Communists; we opposed both in principle, but we fought them
in a purely personal-political sense; they were the nuisances who
disrupted our meetings and conferences. In the I.L.P., with our
'critical support for the Soviet Union', we were not anti-Com-
munist, but the Stalinists all the same were our political enemies. The Blackshirts we did not take very seriously; the movement
attracted the so-called anti-Semites, and it had a certain amount
of support in High Society—we used to refer to 'upper-class
Fascists'—but it had no broad following among the mass of
people. The use of shirts as uniform for a political organisation,
and the wearing of high boots, was altogether too un-English.

Sinclair Lewis published a novel that year entitled, *It Can't
Happen Here*, to show that it could. Only, of course, Sinclair
Lewis's 'here' was America, not old England. His *Main Street*
and *Babbitt*, in the Twenties, made more impression on us. Or
so I think. They were anyhow more talked about. He was,
really, the supreme 'propaganda' novelist; we had our own
propaganda novelists, but no one anywhere near approaching
his stature. Whether one liked his work or not, stylistically, as
literature, there was no disputing the fact that he was a giant.

In the theatre we had propaganda in the shape of Greenwood's *Love on the Dole*, and for culture Eliot's *Murder in the
Cathedral*. The outstanding event in the theatre that year, however, for some of us—indeed for very many of us—was *Romeo
and Juliet* at the New Theatre, with Peggy Ashcroft as Juliet
and John Gielgud and Laurence Olivier alternating as Romeo.
We were, of course, passionately partisan; I was always a Gielgud girl myself. For me he brought the essential poetry to the
part, incomparably.

A play in which I had a special interest was Laurence Housman's *Victoria Regina*, done that year at the little Gate Theatre, then 'under the arches' at Charing Cross; Pamela Stanley
played the Queen and the play was a tremendous success, play-

ing simultaneously in London, Paris and New York. Helen
Hayes played the lead in New York. The play had a special interest for me as Laurence Housman was Reginald's great friend,
always referred to, affectionately, as 'Uncle Laurence'; he was
also in a sense Reginald's patron, for when, at the age of seventy,
he at last achieved success in financial terms, he was so afraid he
might die a rich man, which he would have considered shame-
ful, that in one of his attempts at getting rid of the money as
fast as it rolled in he financed the struggling young Quaker-
poet-pacifist, as Reginald has himself told in his autobiography.

Victoria Regina was a collection of one-act plays which, having been refused a licence by the Lord Chamberlain, could not
be put on in the West End; it was first produced, therefore, at
the Gate, which was a small theatre club. It was not licensed
for West End production until the end of 1936—by the inter-
vention of Edward VIII—one of the last acts of his brief reign.
As Reginald wrote, 'When King George V went to Heaven,
accompanied unobtrusively by Rudyard Kipling and Comrade
Saklatvala (the Communist M.P.) the new King was a stumb-
ling block to many—particularly, as somebody remarked, to
Honest Stan *qui mal y pense*. One man, however, had high
hopes of Edward VIII; and that man was Laurence Housman.'

His hopes were fulfilled in that sensational first week in December, 1936, in which the Crystal Palace was burned down,
and Edward announced that he would marry Mrs. Simpson . . .
and the Housman plays about his grandmother were licensed.
Laurence Housman observed to Reginald shortly afterwards,
when they met at Victoria Station—it would have to be Victoria!—both of them seeing someone off to India—'Jawaharlal Nehru, I think, or it might have been Verrier Elwin,'
Reginald wrote—'the Victorian age is over at last!'

In 1935, however, we took our unlicensed pleasure at the
Gate Theatre and felt rather daring.

We had, too, that summer, the first of Ivor Novello's spectacular musicals, *Glamorous Night*. I had admired him since
his first play—which was also his first production—*The Rat*,
a romantic melodrama of the Paris underworld, done in London in 1923. He played the Apache of the title rôle himself, with

lovely Isabel Jeans—she of the swan neck—as his leading lady.
It was melodramatic nonsense, I suppose, but I have remembered it vividly down through the years. I saw him in his last
musical, *King's Rhapsody*, in which he was playing a few hours
before his sudden death in 1951. That, too, was romantic nonsense, but Novello had, then, as much in the way of looks and
what we now call charisma as in the Twenties. But he had much
more, I think—talent that amounted almost to genius, and I
agree with Paul Tanqueray, who considers him the English
counterpart of Franz Lehár and that the music of both will
always be played.

In December, 1935, Ramon Novarro, the great romantic
star of the silent screen, arrived in London, to play in a musical
at His Majesty's Theatre, *A Royal Exchange,* with Doris
Kenyon. He was mobbed by his fans on arrival, but the show
only lasted a week or two, and has been described as the 'theatrical disaster of that or any other year'. Poor handsome
Novarro; he didn't do much after the advent of the 'talkies',
though he did play opposite Greta Garbo in *Mata Hari* in 1931.
In recent years, his looks having gone—he was born in 1899—
he played character parts on television, and very successfully.
In 1969, it may be recalled, he was found brutally murdered
in his bed in his home in California. Two young men were subsequently convicted. Novarro had the reputation of being what
the Americans call 'gay'. . . .

His great success, I suppose, after *Scaramouche* in 1923, was
his version of *Ben Hur* in 1929, generally considered the better
of the two versions, and certainly the most successful.

But to return to 1935, and the theatre : there was the 'young
Welsh actor', Emlyn Williams, in his own play, *Night Must
Fall*, and to this day I recall, with the authentic shiver down
the spine, the slamming of the front door when the domestic
help—I think it was—left, and there was the frightening realisation that the elderly woman—Dame May Whitty—was now
alone in the house with the young killer, Emlyn Williams. There
are very few plays one remembers in this way after a lapse of
thirty-five years.

There were some memorable films that year, too—*The*

Thirty-nine Steps, with Robert Donat and Madeleine Carroll; Paul Robeson in *Sanders of the River*, and Grace Moore singing sweetly in *One Night of Love*. We had Bette Davis and Leslie Howard in Maugham's *Of Human Bondage*, and Victor Maclagen in Liam O'Flaherty's *The Informer*. And Garbo in *Anna Karenina*—unforgettably.

That summer the first Penguins were published, at sixpence. They included Mary Webb's *Gone to Earth* and Hemingway's *A Farewell to Arms*. The previous year I had sat in a Piccadilly pub with the Lane brothers, Allen, Richard, John; they had a cardboard model of a penguin, with which they fooled about, waddling it along the table at which we sat; they were laughing, yet deadly serious. 'Our idea was paperbacks at sixpence, and calling them Penguins,' Allen said. I inquired, through a ginny haze, 'Why Penguins?' They laughed and demanded, 'Why not?' To which there was no logical answer. I asked if they had any money. About two hundred pounds each in the Post Office, they said, lightly.

John was killed in World War II, in the Navy; Richard went to Australia; and as I write this Allen is newly dead after two operations for cancer. He died titled and a millionaire, but it wasn't only the sixpenny Penguins that did that for him, but the five-bob *Lady Chatterley* of 1960, after the failure of the prosecution . . . a literary event which opened the floodgates to the deluge of pornography which now engulfs us.

There was a book prosecution in 1935, too—of a novel about life in a cargo ship, entitled, *Boy*, by James Hanley. The boy of the title was the cabin boy, sexually molested by one of the crew. The novel was prosecuted for the homosexual passages, of which, as I remember it, there were only one or two, and done without any of the clinical detail fashionable in fiction today. However, a policeman in Bury read the book from a library three years after its publication, was shocked, considered it obscene, and secured a conviction. Fantastically, the book is still not in the British Museum Catalogue, which means that it is on their banned list and has to be specially asked for. In the B.M. Catalogue there appears the following: *Summary report of the*

*police proceedings against the directors and firm of Boriswood,
Ltd., in regard to the book entitled* Boy, *written by James Hanley. 1935.* I had a copy of the novel when it was first published,
and wish I still had it, for it is now very 'rare'. I remember being moved by it, and though it was startling at the time to read
of homosexual incidents, clearly stated, there was nothing in-
decent about it. It was 'brutal realism', in the Hanley manner,
and not more shocking than other descriptions of harsh reality.
The publishers and author of the novel were heavily fined and
warned that they were 'liable to prosecution for every copy of
the book in circulation'. The National Council for Civil Liberties took up the case, but were not able to do anything or get
the law changed. The case did, however, arouse interest in the
activities of the Council.

In retrospect, in spite of some good plays and films—there was
nothing remarkable in literature except for Sinclair Lewis's
It Can't Happen Here, and Hanley's *Boy*—1935 was a silly
sort of year, with its Jubilee euphoria and its refusal to see the
writing on the wall. Lloyd George was discussing world affairs
in a series of newspaper articles syndicated to America and
declaring that Hitler had 'given the whole world a statesmanlike
lead', and brushing off European fears of war with the assertion
that France with her new fortresses—the Maginot Line—was
immune from attack.

   In England the War Office inaugurated A.R.P.—Air Raid
Precautions, the forerunner of Civil Defence; that is to say the
A.R.P. Bill was presented in Parliament, though in fact not
passed until 1937. The Red Cross gave volunteers first-aid and
anti-gas training, and there was some training in the naval area
at Portsmouth; also some War Office tests were carried out at
Chislehurst, but there was very little general interest until 1937;
in 1935 we did not really believe in the likelihood of World War
II. After all, the War Office had been discussing Air Raid Precautions ever since 1924.

   More interesting to the man-in-the-street were the new-style
police emerging from the new Metropolitan Police College
opened by the Prince of Wales the previous year. Lord

Trenchard's young gentlemen with public school educations. The innovation was regarded with a combination of amusement and impatience. The 'gentleman bobby' was a break with British tradition; our police had always been recruited from the lower-middle and working classes, and this, for some reason, had seemed to us right and proper—*natural*. We did not want them with B.B.C. voices; the cultural accents of the B.B.C. were all right in their place, but who wants a classy copper?

Various ribald jokes were current, but in some quarters there was also a certain amount of resentment over this invasion of the élite into the police ranks. It was even considered sinister—fascistic. The class element came into it; ex-Servicemen were to be servants at the new college, and the young gents would dine at 8 p.m. wearing dinner-jackets; and wear mufti when off duty. It was not our idea of coppers, but it was all anyhow of more interest than A.R.P.

Nineteen-thirty-five, too, was the year of Recovery; there were still two million unemployed, but the figures were nevertheless the lowest in years. By the end of the year, also, Mosley's movement had more or less petered out; there were no candidates from the British Union of Fascists in the November election.

In the feminine world there was a craze for bare legs among girls and younger women, and red hair was fashionable in the autumn; the theatrical producer, Tom Arnold, declared that the 'red-haired girl will be in the front line of all pantomimes this Christmas', adding that the demand for red-haired girls was much greater than the supply. I had not cut off my hair in the Twenties and I did not henna it in the Thirties; the bare-legged craze is hard to understand, for the hemline was low again, almost down to the ankle, even with suits.

In the masculine world there was a minor outbreak of beards, and as a consequence an absurd new game called 'Beaver' became popular; people went beaver-spotting in the way schoolboys now go train-spotting; if you saw a man wearing a beard you shouted 'Beaver!' and scored a point. Countering this was a Secret Society of Beavers, the members of which undertook not to appear barefaced and to be revenged upon anyone who laughed at beards. The society named King George V and Bernard Shaw as outstanding examples of men whose appearance was improved by a beard. Reginald Reynolds in his scholarly but very amusing book, *Beards,** cites Partridge's *Dictionary of Slang* (1937) as mentioning the word 'beaver' for a bearded man or a beard, and as 'a passing term and pastime of the 1920's'.

Reginald, in *Beards,* called the Twenties and Thirties the 'Indian Summer between the two world wars', and says that his 'one clear nostalgic memory will always be the films of Charlie Chaplin in the Twenties. Here the toothbrush moustache reached its peak of absurdity; and it is curious to reflect that the much imitated Chaplin moustache, two short smudges below the nose, was another example of Nature imitating Art, for the moustache of Mr. Chaplin was a false one. Among those who copied this preposterous style was a certain Herr Hitler (described in the *Encyclopedia Britannica*, 14th edition, in the article on Bavaria, as "a good demagogue but no politician") who achieved the incredible feat of persuading the German people to take his paranoia seriously, in spite of his vaudeville appearance.'

Whether in England in 1935 we were taking the funny little man in Germany with the Charlie Chaplain moustache seriously is a moot point; we were and we weren't. Charles Duff in his chapter on England and the two world wars, in his book, *England and the English*, says that 'we are still too close to events to be able to analyse them with detachment. Did we or did we not in the 1930's realise the significance of the rise of Hitler? No doubt the experts did. But the man in the street? Hitler was still rather a joke to him; Mussolini was a clown. Not until the Spanish War of 1936–8 clarified the position—and gave more than an inkling that from the point of view of Hitler and Mussolini it was the prelude to another world war—did the English begin to realise that they must face another great trial. It came in 1939.'

Certainly to me in Moscow, in that autumn of 1935, the Abyssinian War, which had so worried me before I set out,

* 1950. Published in U.S.A., 1949.

seemed remote. The days were spent in exhausting struggles with officials in the attempt to get permits for Turkestan, and the nights at the theatre. I found Moscow much changed since my first visit in 1934; it had become 'Americanised'. I wrote, in *South to Samarkand*, 'Where had been tangles of scaffolding a year ago now stand great palaces of commerce, industry, education, blocks of apartments, a vast new hotel, a vast new library; gone is the church with the blue dome with the golden stars, gone the last vestige of the Chinese Wall. . . .'

The Bolshoi Theatre no longer looked across a square with trees and shrubberies, for the Theatre Square gardens had been practically abolished to make a car park and taxi rank. But there were still flower-sellers at street corners, offering dahlias, carnations, asters, and there was an absence of the begging children who had hung round the theatres and big hotels during the Theatre Festival. In the public park old women swept up the leaves, and children played with the big plane leaves, arranging them in flat golden bunches, making crowns of them with a kite's tail down the back. Outside the city, in the countryside, the birches were golden, the landscape gently undulating, and there were small wooden chalet-like houses and the onion-shaped domes of village churches—remnants of pre-revolutionary Russia.

I had, it seems, in 1935, a kind of love-hate relationship with the U.S.S.R., perpetually torn between admiration and exasperation, respect and mistrust. 'By night over the Kremlin flies a floodlit red flag', I wrote. 'It licks against the darkness of the sky like a flame when the wind stirs it, and has all the exciting beauty of fire . . . It moved me as the red flag at the bows of the Soviet ship in which I travelled to Leningrad had moved me. As a symbol of its own violent poetry; all the fanatic passion of the revolutionary is in its flame . . . then back at the hotel I would watch the better-off Russians dancing, drinking, supping, and be unable to resist the thought which in imagination hauled the flag down to half-mast and imposed a vast question-mark over the face of the new Russia—the thought : What have these people to do with the old women who sweep leaves in the streets and parks, with the drab figures who pass in and out of the

dark noisome doorways of tenement buildings in which humanity huddles together, fobbed off with jam tomorrow in lieu of
the bread-and-circuses of capitalist countries? So many people
in this great Americanised, almost feverishly progressive city,
very nearly smartly dressed, and so many still very nearly in
rags . . . Is the whole community in this forward movement, or
are these better-dressed people merely the nucleus of a new
middle-class?'

Reflections and questions in Stalin's Russia in the autumn
of 1935. I don't know the answers; I have never been back, and
I have no opinions regarding the 'bourgeois trends in the Soviet
Union'. People go there nowadays on package holidays, and
Samarkand is included; you can send postcards home from
Red Russia as from anywhere else—I have received some, and
the senders seemed to think they were getting their money's
worth. It was a nice trip, they say when they get back, all very
interesting, but the people on the streets seemed drab . . . so may-
be it isn't much different from thirty-five years ago.

I had my thirty-fifth birthday in Russia, but where I do not
remember. It was probably on a train; wherever it was I have
no doubt it was toasted with vodka.

In September, shortly before leaving for Russia, my third
volume of short stories, *The Falconer's Voice*, dedicated to
Donia Nachshen, had been published; it is sad that having survived the arduous illegal Turkestan journey together our
friendship did not survive the book that came out of it. It was
a very great disappointment to me that she would not allow
her splendid sketches to illustrate the book, which she regarded
as anti-Soviet, but she was a dedicated Communist, and across
the years I can respect her stand more than, I think, I did at
the time. People must do what seems right to them—and she
did.

In the spring of that year Paul Tanqueray had a very
successful exhibition of his photographs at his Dover Street
studio; T. W. Earp, reviewing it in the *Daily Telegraph*, wrote
of Paul Tanqueray's 'craftsmanship and art', and declared that
his work took a 'high place in this country among the productions of the modern movement'.

The Jubilee Year closed with a New Year's Eve dance at the Grosvenor Hotel, London, at which nearly fifteen hundred guests danced to a band conducted at midnight by eight-year-old Master Johnnie Hoban, described as the son of a public-school master. It was reported that in other hotels and restaurants 'children as young as three will stay up late to entertain guests and make entrances at midnight'. At the Savoy Hotel there was a giant hour-glass, so arranged that its sands ran out precisely at midnight, when trumpeters of the Life Guards appeared and greeted 1936 with a fanfare.

The sands were running out all right, but not just for the close of 1935; they were running out for the end of an era.

19

Finale and Prelude

King George V, the 'sailor king', as the Press liked to describe him, died on January 6, 1936. I wrote in my second volume of autobiography, *Privileged Spectator*, 'A number of men had been killed in a pit disaster about that time, but as news and tragedy it could not compete with the death-in-bed of the amiable old gentleman who collected stamps and, so far as the masses who "mourned" him were concerned, had the negative virtue of never having done anyone any harm.'

I was in hospital at the time for treatment for intestinal trouble which had followed a bout of dysentery in Turkestan and was impatient of nurses who came off night duty and instead of going to bed went off to queue up for admission to Westminster Hall to see the dead king lying in state. I still find it strange that people should wish to do this, but it no longer exasperates me; the North Country saying applies—'There's nowt so strange as folks.' And *chacun à son goût*. People do more foolish things, and worse things. He was a good king, I suppose, as kings go.

The Pure Flame was published that month, and I began work on *South to Samarkand*. I finished it in May and then went to Switzerland with my daughter. On my return I drafted a light-weight novel I entitled, *Women Also Dream*, which I described at the time as 'the story of an Ella-Maillart-Freya-Stark-Amelia-Earhart sort of woman, who, like her creator, could not rest from travel'. I had met the Swiss traveller, Ella

Maillart, before going to Russia, and immensely admired her book, *Turkestan Solo*. I did not meet Amelia Earhart, America's 'Lady Lindy', but her flying exploits fired my imagination. She had flown the Atlantic solo in 1928, and in 1935 had flown the Pacific from Honolulu to Oakland, California, in a 2400-mile hop, the first solo flight made by anyone from Hawaii to the U.S. coast. There was a great deal of interest in this sort of adventure in the Thirties. In 1930 we had had Amy Johnson's solo flight to Australia, and we had had Jim Mollison's sensational London–Cape flight—after which he married Amy Johnson. In 1933 there was their joint record-breaking flight across the Atlantic. But it was Amelia Earhart who was in the news in 1935, and equated in my mind with adventurous travellers such as Ella Maillart and Freya Stark, and it was of such a woman that, newly returned from my own adventure, I wanted to write.

I worked on the book in a Sussex pub and later in the convent, where I also corrected the proofs of *South to Samarkand*. The novel was designed to offset some of the heavy socialist propaganda of *Cactus* and *The Pure Flame*; it was written, I suppose, in a reaction against the Soviet Union, for the 1935 journey had proved bitterly disillusioning. I used to say, wrily, on my return that I was critical of the U.S.S.R. not because it was a Communist country but because it wasn't.

But the Left intelligentsia still ardently supported it, and May, 1936, saw the founding of Victor Gollancz's immensely successful Left Book Club—it quickly built up a membership of some forty thousand members. Its title was misleading, for there was more to the Left than Communism, but the so-called Left Book Club was Marxist—not exclusively but predominantly. A Labour Book Club and a Socialist Book Club set up in opposition could not compete; Marxist orientation was intellectually fashionable.

It should be recorded, however, that the publishing house of Secker and Warburg were publishing a series of Left books at that time which did not conform to the popular line of Left orthodoxy represented by Victor Gollancz and the Left Book Club. They published a book by the West Indian Trotskyist,

C. L. R. James, and a book by another West Indian, George Padmore, a renegade from the Communist fold, and a book by a bearded Kenyan called Jomo Kenyatta....

They asked Reginald if he would like to write for them about India, and commissioned the book he was to entitle, *The White Sahibs in India*, which was published in 1937 with a foreword by his friend Jawaharlal Nehru. It was his first book, and he wrote it whilst still working full time for the No More War Movement. In his autobiography he says of the book that when he looks at its bulk 'and the terrifying phalanges of footnotes' he wonders how he completed the work whilst doing a full-time job. That he did so was certainly an achievement, like the massively documented work itself.

In the year in which Secker and Warburg published Reginald's *White Sahibs* they commissioned a non-fiction work from me, *Women and the Revolution*, which was published in 1938. It was dedicated to Emma Goldman; the dedication took the form of a Dedicatory Letter, written in October 1937, whilst the Spanish Civil War was still being waged; a large part of the long chapter on Russian revolutionary women was, of course, about her. When the Spanish Civil War broke out in July, 1936, it was natural that she, the veteran anarchist, should go to Spain, since more than the anti-Fascist struggle against General Franco was involved in that war; there was also —although it was not generally understood—the anarchist re- volutionary struggle, which opposed both Franco and the Republican-Communist alliance. In Catalonia in 1936 Emma found, as she wrote to me, the ideas and ideals she had cherished for fifty years and more—she was then sixty-seven—'in actual bloom, holding out the promise of golden fruit for the masses in Spain'. She had but one thought at that time—to end her years in Spain, to dedicate every moment of the rest of her life to the work there, the serving of the revolution, the building of a new free life. She had lived to see the great anarchist dream of liberty in process of realisation....

Considerable progress was in fact made by the anarchists in Catalonia; transport and various industries were collectivised, there were agricultural collectives, and Catalonia conducted its affairs along anarcho-syndicalist lines, without reference to the Valencia government. I have told the story of it in full in *Women and the Revolution*, in the chapter devoted to the Spanish Revolution, and there is a considerable literature on the Spanish Civil War, though not all of it explains the anarchist revolutionary struggle behind the anti-Fascist struggle. Secker and Warburg published an excellent little book, *Red Spanish Notebook*, by Juan Brea and Mary Low, in 1937. It covers the first six months of the Civil War and the Revolution. In 1936 they published, also, Dr. Edward Conze's book, *Spain Today*, which gives a concise outline of the events leading up to July, 1936. In 1936, also, there was a very good novel by the Spanish author, Ramon Sender, *Seven Red Sundays*, which is about the Revolution, some conflicts in the struggle, and revolutionary Spanish women. The Revolution was crushed by the Barcelona Rising in May, 1937, and, heart-broken but not defeated, Emma Goldman came to London to campaign to the British people, whom she despised for their non-intervention, and raise money from them for 'arms for Spain'. Into this campaign I was roped : Reginald, as a Gandhi man and a Quaker, would have no part in it, though his sympathies were all with the Spanish anarchists in their objectives. We had both by then undergone a process of conversion to anarchism as a political philosophy, disillusioned by then, as we both were, with all governments and all political parties. Why we nevertheless remained members of the Independent Labour Party for a few more years I don't really know, unless it was that we felt that the I.L.P. was more likely to bring about the social revolution in England than were the anarchists, who had even less following. Reginald left the party in 1939, after sweeping out of the Annual Conference in anger and disgust, after failing to get a vote of censure passed on John McGovern, one of the executive council, 'whose anti-Arab speeches in Parliament (after the Zionists had invited him to Palestine and made a big fuss of him) had disgusted many in his own party'. I left the party myself a little later, over their support, for me not sufficiently critical, of the U.S.S.R.

But in the summer of 1936, despite our strong anti-Franco

feeling—which was the feeling of the intelligentsia in general—
we were not caught up in any Spanish War activities—that was
to come the following year, for me with the arrival of Red
Emma in London, for Reginald with the arrival of four thousand evacuated Basque children at Southampton, when he was
one of a handful of people whose job it was to get them housed
—in pouring rain—in a reception camp of bell tents at Stone-
ham. He has told the fantastic story in his autobiography. There
were wry jokes about 'Basqueing in the rain', for the rain went
on for a week.

In 1936, however, there was nothing we could usefully do,
and we were not being pushed into anything, though the com-
munistic international Left moved quickly on behalf of anti-
Franco Spain—but not on behalf of the Revolution—and am-
bulances were subscribed for, equipped, and sent out, together
with medical units, and meetings were organised and collections
taken. Young men rushed off to join the International Brigade,
composed of non-Spanish anti-Francoists. George Orwell was
one of the first of the anti-Fascist foreigners to arrive in Spain;
he was there in December, 1936. He says in his splendid book,
Homage to Catalonia, published in 1938 by Secker and Warburg, that he had gone there with the idea of writing newspaper
articles, but had joined the militia almost immediately, 'because
at that time and in that atmosphere it seemed the only conceiv-
able thing to do. The Anarchists were still in virtual control of
Catalonia and the revolution was still in full swing.' Ralph Fox
was one of those who died fighting in Spain; at the time
I thought it a tragic waste of a talented young writer and a very
likeable young man, since it was never fighting men the Spanish
anti-Fascists were short of, but arms; now I don't know; he did
what he had to do, and a man cannot die better than in the service of an ideal. Esmond Romilly—who married Jessica Mit-
ford—joined the International Brigade and survived the fighting, only to die in 1941, in the R.A.F., in a raid over Hamburg.

As I remember it, the talk in the summer of 1936 was all of
the Spanish Civil War, and people and the Press were passionately partisan. The *Morning Post* existed then and was strongly
pro-Franco, as was the *Daily Mail*; the *News Chronicle* was as

strongly Republican. In the literary world most people were anti-Franco—a survey was published by the *Left Review* in June, 1937, 'Authors Take Sides'. It makes very interesting reading. Only two authors hoped for an anarcho-syndicalist regime with the defeat of Franco: Herbert Read, who was an avowed anarchist, and myself. Read declared that 'in Spain, and almost only in Spain, there still lives a spirit to resist the bureaucratic tyranny of the State and the intellectual intolerance of all doctrinaires'. A few authors were neutral: Vera Brittain as a pacifist; Ezra Pound declared 'Spain is an emotional luxury to a gang of sap-headed dilettantes'; Seàn O'Faolain was neutral because, he said, Fascism was 'lousy' and so was Communism, and he had apparently not heard of any alternatives; T. S. Eliot felt that 'at least a few men of letters' should remain above the strife; H. G. Wells was neutral asserting that the 'real enemy is not the Fascist but the Ignorant Fool'. Lady Eleanor Smith declared herself a 'warm adherent of General Franco'—on humanitarian grounds, she quaintly said. Evelyn Waugh avowed that were he a Spaniard he would be fighting for General Franco, but that as an Englishman he was not in the predicament of choosing between two evils; he was not a Fascist and would never become one unless it were the only alternative to Marxism. His brother, Alec Waugh, was neutral, feeling it not essential for an Englishman to take sides, because he did not accept the argument, ' "It's Spain's turn now. It will be ours tomorrow". Things *are* different here.' Bernard Shaw's opinion was printed as Unclassified; he, also, felt that it was 'not our business', and declared that 'in Spain both the Right and the Left so thoroughly disgraced themselves in the turns they took in trying to govern their country before the Right revolted, that it is impossible to say which of them is the more incompetent. Spain must choose for herself...'

George Graves and Alan Hodge, the authors of *The Long Weekend, a Social History of Great Britain, 1918–1939,** assert categorically of the Spanish Civil War that 'never since the French Revolution had there been a foreign question that so divided intelligent British opinion as this. . . . But though

* 1940.

opinion was divided, the majority felt at least sympathy for the Republic. .... Many people, in fact, who either held progressive views, or simply believed in "decency" supported the Republican side, and many enthusiastic young men fought for it and were killed.'

By the end of the year, however, in England we were talking about something else—'The King and Mrs. Simpson'. The story did not break in the British press until the first week in December, though it had been known to many of us through the American press ever since 1934. When the news broke the great British public couldn't get over it at all; who'd have thought it, and well I never; and fancy! I recorded in *Privileged Spectator*: 'At every street corner, in every 'bus and train, in every shop, on every railway station, wherever men and women talked together you heard the words, "The King" and "Mrs. Simpson"; and there were smiles; everyone looked as though they had just been told a good story—as indeed they had. There was positively a festive air abroad.'

But that was only the day the news broke; after that partisanship took over, and people began to be nervous about asking each other what they thought for fear they should be on the other side—so extraordinarily high did feeling run on this issue. It was as it had been during the Abyssinian War, for and against applying 'sanctions', and as it was over the Spanish War; opinion was sharply divided, but I think it is true to say that in general, among the common people as well as the intelligentsia, there was sympathy for the King. Not to be 'for the King' was to ally oneself with what we called the 'Blimps', personified in 'stuffy old Baldwin', and the Archbishop of Canterbury. It was unfortunate for those of us who were 'for the King' that the British Union of Fascists also was, and printed leaflets saying so.

Edward shut himself up in Fort Belvedere and Mrs. Simpson tactfully went to France. It was said that in Fort Belvedere the King was hitting the bottle good and hard and telling Baldwin where he got off. These rumours afforded satisfaction to those who opposed the King, because they confirmed his unworthiness; but they also afforded satisfaction to those of us who were on his side, because we liked to think of him behaving so humanly. Good old Edward, and down with Stuffy Stan!

There was a great rush to buy the Edward VIII Coronation mugs, and even an inveterate republican such as myself went out and scoured the shops for an Edward VIII calendar because a little maid I had then—we had resident maids right up to the outbreak of war—said we should have one for the kitchen, to show whose side we were on, it being a shame that the King couldn't please himself whom he married. . . .

I found a calendar under a pile of George VI ones which had been rushed into print as soon as Edward had abdicated, which he did on December 10, broadcasting to the nation that he did so because he could not be happy without the woman he loved. I had no radio then—I did not in fact acquire one until 1963, when, having been told of the events in Iraq and the shooting of General Kassim, I rushed and bought a transistor—so did not hear the broadcast, but it was apparently very moving, and the authors of *The Long Weekend* describe it as delivered in 'an angry, tragic, harsh voice'. I remember, however, being moved by the fact that next morning the man who had been King, and immensely popular, left England accompanied only by an equerry and a little dog. I found it strange, and I still do find it strange, that a national figure, *the* national figure, could be replaced overnight, like the merest office boy, and his brother, unknown to the general public, and singularly lacking in charisma, poor man, could be built up to the required image. It only serves to underline, surely, the absurdity of the whole system. But there it was; the year which had begun with George V ended with George VI, with a few months of Edward VIII in between; 1935 was Jubilee Year and 1936 the Year of the Three Kings.

What with all that and the Crystal Palace going up in flames on the night of November 30—a symbol and a sign?—it was quite a year. There was a story current that the Crystal Palace had been set on fire deliberately by order of a Government department because it was a landmark for German bombers in the event of war. Lord Ponsonby, who was a pacifist, told Reginald this in all seriousness. But whatever the cause of its destruction, the end of the old Crystal Palace had a kind of symbolism even at the time; it had always been there, and then overnight it was gone—as the King was to go ten days later. On December 1, those who had not seen the flames in the sky at Sydenham the night before, learned of the destruction of this bit of Victoriana; two days later the Press aired the story of the King and Mrs. Simpson. There was no connection between the two events, yet somehow they did add up to the end of an era—the era which had begun around 1918, developed as the Twenties and overflowed into the Thirties. The Jubilee year was perhaps the final fling, and the burning of the Crystal Palace the spectacular finale.

Nineteen-thirty-six had been a year in which public opinion had been divided in the summer by the outbreak of the Spanish Civil War, and in the winter by the royal romance culminating in the abdication; in between we went to the theatre, and to the cinema, and read books, and caught boat-trains to the Continent; we still asked each other, as in the Twenties; have you been, have you read, have you seen? There were the Noël Coward one-act plays, *Tonight at 8.30*, featuring himself and Gertrude Lawrence; there was Ibsen's *Doll's House*, with, surprisingly, Lydia Lopokova playing as Nora; there was a beautiful production of Max Beerbohm's lovely story, *The Happy Hypocrite*, dramatised by Clemence Dane, with Ivor Novello and Vivien Leigh, and the mask worn by the happy hypocrite to hide his ugliness designed by Angus McBean. For some reason this play which had everything, one would have thought, was a failure. There was a fine production of Chekhov's *The Seagull*, with Gielgud, Stephen Haggard, Peggy Ashcroft, Edith Evans. Sewell Stokes' *Oscar Wilde* made its London debut at the Gate Theatre, with Robert Morley as Wilde. In the cinema we had *Romeo and Juliet* with Leslie Howard and Norma Shearer in the leading rôles, and costumes by Oliver Messel, but this I did not see, having an incurable aversion to filmed versions of Shakespeare's plays. We had Frank Capra's film, *Mr. Deeds Comes to Town*, with Gary Cooper, a film I liked very much. We had, too, Charlie Chaplin's *Modern Times*, the last of his silent films. It is a film which stays in the memory, the tragicomic story of the 'little man' versus the machine. I have always remembered 'Charlie' in the factory, standing at the moving belt making mechanical manual movements and still making them when he had left the machine; it was comic, but it was terrible, too—like so much in the Chaplin films with their implicit social comment. We all raved about *Modern Times*, and rightly, I think; it was artistically and socially a very important film.

Nineteen-thirty-six saw the publication of Ernst Toller's *Letters from Prison,* done by John Lane, the Bodley Head; it is a fat handsome book with numerous illustrations, and the price was 12s. 6d. net . . . far away and long ago that world of 1936. But it was not the Age of Innocence that the Twenties had been; the Indian Summer was almost over. By the end of 1936 General Franco had still not had that Mass in Madrid which was his declared intention, for that indomitable city was still holding out, but increasingly as the Spanish War dragged on it became evident that Spain was being used as the trial ground for Germany and Italy for the major war to come. It was German bombers which totally destroyed the Basque city of Guernica in the summer of 1937.

The Descent to Avernus was rapid after that and has no place in this book, for the era it set out to describe finished with the outbreak of the Spanish Civil War in the summer of 1936. There was no national euphoria after that, and even the Coronation of George VI in May, 1937, could not produce it; a new era had begun; we who were young in the Twenties were no longer young; the dancing years were long over, and who remembered now the songs we sang? Amusingness and gaiety were out—had been out for some time—and social consciences and anxiety were in, and likely to stay.

Even the Thirties, now, have taken on the aura of history-and-old-times. As to the Twenties, they were before the Flood. Which in a sense they were. The Flood that engulfed us in September 1939, after which the world was never the same again. I write this quite without nostalgia. That Indian Summer between the wars is interesting in retrospect—as the present era will be, some fifty years on.

Index